BATTLES IN FOCUS

GETTYSBURG

The stone wall held by Co. H, 69th Pennsylvania, in the centre of the position attacked by Pickett's Division. The rail fences that delayed the Confederate advance on either side of the Emmitsburg Pike can be seen, and the tree line in the distance marks the spot where Pickett's men began their advance.

BATTLES IN FOCUS

GETTYSBURG

PHILIP KATCHER

BRASSEY'S

First published in 2003 by Brassey's

A member of Chrysalis Books plc

Brassey's
The Chrysalis Building, Bramley Road,
London W10 6SP

North American orders:
Casemate Publishing, 2114 Darby Road,
Havertown, PA 19083, USA

Library of Congress Cataloging in Publication
Data available

British Library Cataloguing in Publication Data
A catalogue record for this book is available
from the British Library

ISBN 1 85753 319 4

All photographs unless otherwise indicated:
Chrysalis Images and Author's Collection

Edited and designed by DAG Publications Ltd
Designed by David Gibbons
Edited by Michael Boxall
Cartography by Anthony A. Evans

Printed in Spain.

CONTENTS

INTRODUCTION

While the actual effects of the battle may not justify it, Gettysburg is easily the most popular, written about, and studied battle in American history.

The battle came about by accident. Neither side wanted to fight it. In the midst of the third year of the struggle for Southern independence, Robert Edward Lee's Army of Northern Virginia launched its second invasion of the North in an attempt to relieve pressure on agriculture in the east and troops fighting along the Mississippi River at the same time. Lee wanted to avoid a battle, where his troops would be at a disadvantage with limited munitions available and his line of retreat potentially cut. Meade, the newly-appointed commander of the Union's Army of the Potomac, was cautious. He had to protect Washington and eastern seaboard cities first. He wanted to fight, if necessary, a defensive battle, and in fact had picked a site along Pipe Creek, where formidable natural defensive positions were to be found.

That both sides collided at the cross-roads town of Gettysburg was a fluke, and that Lee's on-the-scene commanders violated his wishes to begin a major battle was unfortunate for him. Neither Lee nor Meade were present as the battle began and grew in intensity. By the time both arrived, the battle seemed inevitable.

After the initial fight, Union troops felt that they had won a tremendous victory. 'Fredericksburg!', defending Union soldiers cried out after repelling Lee's men on 3 July, as if the battle made up for that earlier disaster. Union troops gathered up fallen Confederate colours by the armful, proof of their great victory.

Confederates with Lee's Army, however, felt that it had been a standoff. After all, they held their ground on 4 July, before retiring, and Meade's Union troops made no effort to assault their positions. Lee's Confederates in no way felt that they had suffered a defeat. They had held their ground and bought time for farmers back in Virginia to begin bringing in the crops.

The same feelings were not held elsewhere in the South, however. Civilians saw Lee's men retiring under pressure, no matter how slight, from Pennsylvania, through Maryland, and back into Virginia at the same time as the final Confederate strongholds on the Mississippi, Vicksburg and Port Hudson, fell. Together the Union victories were a crushing blow to Southern morale, and one from which Southern civilians never fully recovered.

At the same time, the combination raised Northern morale to the highest point ever. While Union troops had won victories consistently in the west, most of the mass media, such as *Harper's Weekly* magazine, were based in the east, in New York, and eastern war news was dominant. War news in the east had never been good for the Union cause. True, the Army of the Potomac had forced Lee's troops off Maryland soil a year earlier at Antietam, but only at great cost in the bloodiest single day of the war, and most observers considered the battle actually a draw, with a bit of an edge actually going to the Confederates. After that came the disaster at Fredericksburg, the embarrassing 'Mud March' along the Rappahannock, Lee's greatest victory of the war at the Second Manassas, and the huge defeat by Lee's grossly outnumbered Confederates at Chancellorsville. Lee and his men looked invincible. Gettysburg proved that they weren't.

In later years, Union veterans made the field at Gettysburg more of a shrine than any other battle site. Almost every unit that served there placed at least one memorial on the field on some position where they claimed, often amidst fierce controversy that even ended up in court rooms, they had fought. Union veterans made many pilgrimages to the site, and eventually they were joined by Confederate veterans at the 50th Anniversary encampment there. Such encampments served to keep Gettysburg in the public eye.

The Southerners lost the war and spent less time after the war memorialising what they had done. In many ways they were so busy trying to revive their economy after the war, they couldn't do so even if that had been their intention. Fewer Confederate veterans, in terms of a percentage of all who served and were eligible, joined veterans' organisations than did Union veterans.

Even so, Gettysburg was not forgotten in the South. The battle became a major Southern veteran controversy, as those intent on turning Lee into the undefeatable, perfect general, had to explain his loss there. They picked on one of his corps commanders, James Longstreet, who not only condemned in print at least three times Lee's tactics on that field as being the reason for his defeat, but also turned his coat to become a Republican after the war. It was Longstreet, Lee's apologists claimed, who lost the battle because of his slowness in attacking on 2 July and again on the 3rd. The fact that Longstreet claimed that he opposed the attack on 3 July and then it was launched only in the afternoon rather than early in the morning, when the Confederate attack on the Union right began, seemed to back up their claim. Both sides fought in the media for years, bringing more attention to Gettysburg.

So Gettysburg stayed in the public eye from the moment the last shot was fired. Veterans wrote books about what they had done there, and this flow of books has lasted up to the present day. In fact, a modern novel based on the battle, *Killer Angels*, won a Pulitzer Prize and was made into a motion picture.

1

THE WAR PRIOR TO GETTYSBURG

In June 1863, the Confederate high command had a serious problem. It was facing two virtually separate wars, one in the east and the other in the west, and the two were going differently.

The war began in the east with the First Manassas in 1861, an unexpectedly huge Confederate victory in which invading Federal forces expected an easy drive to and capture of Richmond, Virginia. Richmond was vital to the Southern cause. It was their capital, chosen rather than the Confederacy's first capital, Montgomery, Alabama, for political reasons. Virginians had originally been lukewarm on the question of Southern states leaving the United States as a result of the election of an anti-slavery president in 1860. The state's population only voted to join its fellow Southern states when the new Federal administration, led by Illinois' Abraham Lincoln, called for volunteers to 'put down the rebellion' in the South. As with many states that had not originally joined the Southern Confederacy, Virginia's governor said that he would not provide troops for this purpose, and popular feelings against the call to arms led to secession.

Richmond, apart from being a political head of the Confederacy, was also the major industrial city in an otherwise agrarian region. New Orleans, an equally industrialised city, fell to Northern naval attacks in 1862. Although some manufacturers managed to pack up their machinery and move into Georgia, much industrial capability was lost with that city's fall. Likewise, Nashville, Tennessee, another city with a respectable industrial capability, was captured by Federal forces in 1862. Richmond, with its huge Tredegar Iron Works whose facilities were capable of producing cannon, naval armour plating, and iron for railways, was the South's last major industrial centre.

Of course, as in pre-war days, Southerners could sell agricultural products, notably cotton and, to a lesser extent, tobacco, overseas and thereby buy needed cannon, small arms, and other necessary items. But in an initial misguided attempt to get European powers to crash through the blockade of Southern ports declared by Union officials, at first cotton was not allowed to be shipped overseas. By the time the error of this policy was perceived, the small Federal Navy had grown to the point where the blockade had become very effective. While some cotton was indeed shipped overseas and sold to buy weapons and equipment of war, there was never enough to meet all the Southern war needs. Moreover, the government realised that feeding its citizens and soldiers was more important than obtaining foreign weapons, and ordered much land that had been planted with cotton and tobacco to be switched to vegetables and wheat. So local manufacturers had to bear the brunt of producing weapons, ammunition, clothing, and everything needed to maintain a 19th-century army in the field. This meant that Richmond had to be defended to the last.

At the same time, Richmond became a symbol of Southern independence, and rebellion in the North. The mass media, in particular the *New York Tribune* with its national circulation, called for the capture of Richmond from the first. Hence the drive that ended at the First Manassas in 1861. After the failure of that drive, Lincoln brought a successful general from Western Virginia, George B. McClellan, to Washington to reorganise the troops there and prepare them for battle.

McClellan was a genius at turning raw units into combat-ready forces. During the winter of 1861/62 he held countless parades, mock battles, and drills for his men. The Army of the Potomac, as the eastern Federal army was called, became a force to be reckoned with, but McClellan was unwilling to put it to the test. Seemingly not a very brave individual, he projected his own character on his army. Lincoln wanted the army to move in the Spring, even ordering all Federal forces to start a drive south on George Washington's Birthday in February 1862, an order aimed at McClellan.

McClellan did not obey. He disliked the plan of attack favoured by Lincoln and Irwin McDowell, commander of the Army of the Potomac at the First Manassas. It called for an over-land march straight from Washington south to Richmond. It was not a long drive as the crow flies, but the army would have to march, not fly, across river after river that ran west to east. Each river formed a potential Confederate defensive line. Furthermore there were large wooded areas that would be difficult to get through and helpful to the Confederates. Finally, McClellan, either deliberately or unconsciously, projected figures showing the Confederate army to be numerically far greater than was the case. Indeed, his figures, provided in large part by agents of Allan Pinkerton, a civilian railway detective turned intelligence chief, showed the Confederates to far outnumber his own army. The reverse was actually true.

McClellan decided to try a new way of attacking Richmond. He would embark his troops in ships and bring them down to the Virginia coast. There, Fortress Monroe, in the Chesapeake Bay, had never fallen to Virginian forces and was still garrisoned by US Army soldiers. Given the Northern naval superiority, he could land his troops on the tip of the peninsula bounded by the James and York Rivers. Intelligence reports said that the ground was good and hard; he could quickly march up this poorly defended peninsula right into Richmond before the Confederates could reinforce the city.

Lincoln was greatly concerned about this plan because it exposed Washington to any Confederate raid. Therefore he detained a number of McClellan's troops so as to ensure that the city was adequately garrisoned. Having done this, he gave McClellan permission to attack via the Peninsula. Of course, McClellan, incapable of accepting responsibility for the consequences of his own actions, now had a reason to blame others if the project failed, since his numbers would be smaller than projected. And it seems that in his heart McClellan expected anything he planned to fail.

His plan began to unravel almost immediately after his troops landed. The ground that his engineers had said was firm enough to bear artillery easily, turned out to be sandy. The outnumbered defenders, led by an old Regular US Army man, John Bankhead Magruder, known as 'Prince John' because of his extravagant dress and behaviour, put up a more serious fight than McClellan expected. Basing their defensive lines on old ones dug by British troops during the Revolutionary War of 1783 around Yorktown and stretches of water that formed natural defences, the Confederates had a line of fortifications that McClellan considered serious indeed. Moreover, the Confederates concealed their small numbers by marching the same units around again and again, while locomotive whistles blew in the background. McClellan fell for the subterfuge.

McClellan had been an official American Army observer at Sebastopol in the Crimean War, and he now ordered a formal siege as he had seen the allies do there. His troops dug in while artillerymen painfully hauled up huge cannon and mortars for a formal attack. However, on the day he decided to begin the siege his men discovered that the Confederates had already retreated. But the Confederate high command had been able to take advantage of the time Magruder's tactics had bought to reinforce the Peninsula, now under command of General Joseph E. Johnston.

McClellan's men began an advance on Richmond, fighting a fierce scrap at Williamsburg before reaching a point where they could see the city's church spires. At this point Johnston, noted for bad luck in being often wounded in the old Regular US Army, struck. His attack was indecisive, and he was wounded yet again and forced to surrender command of the army. A staff officer from Richmond, Robert E. Lee, was brought in to assume command of the force he now named the Army of Northern Virginia.

Lee's selection was interesting. He was not the first choice; that had gone to a superior officer, G. W. Smith, one of the notable officers in the pre-war Regular US Army. Smith, however, could not take the pressure and apparently had a nervous breakdown under the responsibility. Lee was next highest ranking general locally available and received the job. Initially his men were not happy about it. Lee had a fine record in the Mexican War, where he was a high ranking engineer on the staff of the American commander, Winfield Scott, in the drive on Mexico City. Thereafter he remained in the Engineers until the formation of the new 2nd US Cavalry Regiment by then Secretary of War Jefferson Davis. Lee became a lieutenant colonel in that regiment. As such he happened to be in Washington in 1859 when abolitionist extremist John Brown attempted to create a slave insurrection by capturing the armoury at Harpers Ferry, Virginia. Lee was sent to this town, not far west from Washington, to organise the capture of this small band of extremists. A young cavalry subaltern, James Ewell Brown (JEB) Stuart, assisted him there.

Scott, remembering Lee from the Mexican War, marked him for high command when the Civil War broke out. Lee, however, secretly accepted command of Virginia's forces as a major general, then resigned his US Army commission. His first service in the war was in West Virginia where he was unable to coordinate the movements of two competing subordinates and that area soon fell to the Federals. He was then sent to organise defences along the southern coast south of Virginia, returning to Richmond as the president's adviser.

McClellan was badly startled by Johnston's attack and decided to switch his base of operations to an area on the James River protected by Malvern Hill. Lee, having reorganised his new command, decided to attack. In a campaign known as the Seven Days battle, Lee threw his troops time and again against the retiring Federals, each time suffering more losses than they did, and the campaign ended at Malvern Hill where an unplanned attack against Federal artillery posted on the crest of the hill cost the Confederates huge losses. But Lee's aggression had totally taken any fight out of McClellan that had ever been there. McClellan now was bottled up in a small post on the James, never again to threaten Richmond.

Lincoln, despairing of any success from the Peninsula, brought another successful western general, John Pope, to Washington. Pope was to take the forces scattered around there and in Western Virginia, merge them into a force known as the Army of Virginia, and march overland towards Richmond along the route Lincoln had originally favoured. Lee, sure of McClellan's inactivity, reacted by moving quickly north. His troops totally fooled Pope as to what they were doing, luring him into wasted attacks on the old field at Manassas. A totally beaten Army of Virginia withdrew to Washington, where it was joined by the Army of the Potomac, which Lincoln ordered to be withdrawn from the Peninsula.

Lee then decided to take the war north to relieve pressure on Virginia farmers and allow them time to bring in their crops peacefully. Splitting his forces into several large groups, he crossed the Potomac River into Maryland in August 1862. Through an unhappy accident, a copy of the orders from his headquarters that detailed how the army was to be split and where the different groups were to go was found by some intelligent Union privates. The orders, minus the cigars around which they had been found wrapped, were sent up to McClellan and immediately seen to be authentic.

McClellan, reacting amazingly quickly for him, drove west to attack Lee's divided force. Confederate forces bought time along the gaps in the mountain range that divide Maryland's east and west, but eventually Lee decided to defend lines around the small town of Sharpsburg, Maryland. McClellan ordered his army to attack, but kept V Corps back in reserve. Staff work was sloppy, however, and the attacks, which began on the Confederate left flank, were uncoordinated. Lee was able to move units from point to point and successfully defended his lines. Towards the end of the day, when Union numbers were finally beginning to tell, a corps led by A. P. Hill, greatly depleted by straggling after its hard march from Harpers Ferry, arrived on the field. With these reinforcements, Lee was able to hold. In fact he even considered attacking next day, but decided against it. McClellan, although his numbers were still superior, did not move, and a day later Lee withdrew his army into Virginia. McClellan followed slowly and the 1862 campaign was essentially over in the east.

Lincoln, finding that McClellan was a failure as a general, replaced him by one of his corps commanders, Ambrose Burnside. He was a genial man who had been trained at the US Military Academy at West Point and then left to become an inventor (of a carbine used by many US cavalrymen) and businessman. He returned to the army as an officer of volunteers and rose to the rank of major general.

Burnside followed Lincoln's plan of an overland assault from Washington to Richmond, but when he reached the Rappahannock River the pontoon bridges he needed had yet to arrive from Washington. He waited for them while Lee fortified the line of ridges above the river bank and the town of Fredericksburg. Only after Lee's lines were fully ready were the bridges in place and Burnside, against the advice of many, launched a frontal assault. Losses were disastrous.

Burnside then tried a march around the Confederate flank, heading west along the river bank. But the bad weather of January 1863 stranded his forces in deep mud, and he was forced to return to his original camps. Lincoln replaced him as commander of the Army of the Potomac with another corps commander, Joseph Hooker.

Hooker was a feisty, red-headed man who lacked the confidence of his fellow corps commanders who believed him to be disloyal to anything and anyone in his way. He planned to follow Burnside's flank march, leaving a force across from Fredericksburg to keep Lee's troops pinned down. In the meantime, spring brought hunger to the Army of Northern Virginia, and Lee was forced to detach Longstreet's Corps to go south to forage and at the same time attempt to free the lower Virginia and North Carolina coast from Federal forces. In May Hooker's men crossed the Rappahannock west of Fredericksburg as Lee's men rushed towards them, leaving only a small force to defend the Fredericksburg line. Hooker had managed to get his men through the heavily wooded area known as the Wilderness when he ran into Lee's forces. At that point he lost his nerve and retired to lines around the Chancellor house, where his larger numbers and superior artillery would be offset by the dense woods.

Lee, ever daring, decided on a major strike. He detached a large element of his force under Stonewall Jackson on a route march around the Federal right flank. Jackson's men hit in the late afternoon and totally routed an entire Federal Corps, the ill-fated and largely foreign-born XI Corps. Only by hard fighting and aided by darkness did the Army of the Potomac stabilise its lines, after Hooker had been removed dazed from the field when a pillar against which he was leaning was struck by a stray cannon-ball.

Reconnoitering along the front that night, Stonewall Jackson was mortally wounded by nervous Confederate troops. Jackson's loss was a major blow to the Confederate Army; time and again he had shown more initiative than any other Confederate field general in finding and striking the enemy's weakest point.

Hooker's army was forced to retreat and return to its earlier camps, there to wait and watch as the Federal army let the initiative pass into Confederate hands.

In the west the war went differently for the Confederates. There, there was no tradition of victory after victory. Kentucky was initially neutral and both sides at first observed this neutrality by not sending troops into the state. This gave a tremendous advantage to the Confederates as it provided a buffer state, so that hundreds of miles of Southern border did not have to be defended by troops. Louisiana Episcopal Bishop turned general Leonidas Polk, however, soon lost this advantage as he, fearing that the Federals would enter the state before him, violated state neutrality by invading it.

Confederate president Jefferson Davis named Albert Sidney Johnston, old 2nd US Cavalry Regiment colonel, thought by many to be the best general the South had, to be overall commander in the western theatre. Johnston seems to have been overwhelmed by the job and made no general strategic plans for the defence of the area. It was, to be honest, a difficult job. While rivers flowed west to east in Virginia, they flowed too often north to south in the west, providing highways for the superior Union naval forces. The Confederates quickly planned forts along these rivers, but these were too often badly designed and manned by untrained and poorly equipped troops.

Fort Henry, one of them built on the Tennessee River, was often under water in any floods, and a Federal naval force, supported by troops under Major General U. S. Grant, quickly took it and then moved to capture Fort Donelson, a short way away on the Cumberland River. With this, Kentucky had been flanked and Tennessee was open to the Federals. Nashville, one of the three major cities in the South, was soon captured. Other naval forces moving up from the Gulf of Mexico, entered the Mississippi River and captured the other major city, New Orleans. The Confederates struck at Grant's army at Shiloh, but failed to destroy his forces; Johnston was killed in the battle and his army was forced to retire to Corinth, Mississippi. The Federals, now commanded by overall theatre commander Henry Halleck, slowly followed and eventually took Corinth.

Island No 10 on the Mississippi fell to Federal forces as point after point was taken from a Confederate force that seemed unable to win a battle. Eventually there were only two Confederate strongholds left on the Mississippi – two strongholds that connected the Trans-Mississippi Department, that included Texas, with the east. Grant was given the job of taking the northern post, Vicksburg, while Major General Nathaniel Banks, a northern politician turned soldier, was given the job of taking Port Hudson.

Grant made several abortive attempts to attack Vicksburg from the north, but eventually decided to take his troops south, past the city, by water, then land and approach from the south. The Confederate commander at Vicksburg, Pennsylvania-born John C. Pemberton, had been ordered to hold the city at all costs. He fell back into the city's line of defences and awaited help from outside as Grant's men set up siege lines. This help was to come from new overall theatre commander Joseph E. Johnston, now recovered from his Peninsula Campaign wounds. Johnston attacked towards Grant's lines, but was met and defeated at Champion's Hill and Jackson, Mississippi. He thereafter fell back and regrouped and re-equipped for another try.

Banks, no soldier really, was able to get siege lines set up around Port Hudson. Several attacks on the city's fortifications failed, and a formal siege began.

This, then, was the situation in which the Confederacy found itself as June 1863 opened. In the west the last strongholds along the vital Mississippi River were severely threatened and if nothing were done, and soon, they looked to be lost. In the east Lee's Army of Northern Virginia easily outfought its enemy at every thrust it made, and the Federals there were now low in morale and confused at the high command level. The question was, what was to be done?

While Davis' main concern was the pressure in his native state of Mississippi, Lee had other problems, chiefly how to feed his army. As early as 27 March 1863, he had written to the Secretary of War: 'The troops of this portion of the army have for some time been confined to reduced rations, consisting of 18 ounces of flour, 4 ounces of bacon of indifferent quality, with occasionally supplies of rice, sugar, or molasses. The men are cheerful, and I received but few complaints; still I don't think it is enough to continue them in health & vigor, and I fear they will be unable to endure the hardship of the approaching campaign. Symptoms of scurvy are appearing among them, and to supply the place of vegetables each regiment is directed to send a daily detail to gather sassafras buds, wild onions, lamb's quarter, & poke sprouts. But for so large an army the supply obtained is very small.' The regulation Confederate ration was a pound of beef or half a pound of bacon and pork and eighteen ounces of bread or flour or twelve ounces of hard bread or a pound and a quarter of corn meal per soldier daily.

Southern food shortages were not confined to Lee's army. Civilians also faced empty grocery shops and butcher stalls throughout the South. Food riots took place in North Carolina and Georgia in March 1863, and on 2 April a mob roamed the streets of Richmond searching for food, but looting other stores as well, until Davis himself and local militia confronted them and forced them to disperse. In a late attempt to solve the problem, Congress passed a joint resolution asking its citizens to stop planting tobacco and cotton in favour of vegetables. On 24 April Congress passed a tax bill calling for payment in food from every farmer and planter in the south, to be delivered to government warehouses for future distribution. Davis published a speech in which he said that there was actually enough meat in the South for everyone, but the roads and railroads were so bad it was difficult to get it to those who needed it.

Transportation was quite a problem. Before the war the South had never had a modern, 19th-century infrastructure. Train lines were short haul for the most part, with different track gauges. Moreover the war had taken a toll of these, as engines, passenger and freight cars, and even track itself could no longer be bought from Northern manufacturers. Mechanics and engineers had been drafted into the Confederate military, reducing the number of qualified train personnel. The Southern train system was slowly being ground into nothingness.

Much of northern Virginia had been fought over and looted for the past two years. Indeed, Union troops occupied it from the Potomac to the Rappahannock Rivers, and such produce and meat as northern Virginia farmers could produce was not available to Confederate troops or civilians. One of the richest farming areas in America, the Shenandoah Valley, had been the scene of much fighting in Stonewall Jackson's famed 'Valley Campaign' only the year before. While the Valley was in Confederate hands for the most part, much damage had been done to farms and crops there and it would take time to repair it all.

Therefore, when the Confederate Army's Commissary General, the much-hated L. B. Northrup, was asked for more food for the Army of Northern Virginia, he supposedly said, 'If General Lee wants rations let him get them from Pennsylvania.'

While it is true that in the east food was a problem, Davis and his Secretary of War, James Sedden, saw the war in the west as a greater problem. The solution to that problem they felt, before meeting with Lee, would be to send some of the Army of Northern Virginia's troops to reinforce the Army of Tennessee under General Braxton Bragg, to help Johnston break through Union siege lines at Vicksburg. While any general is loath to see troops taken from him, even some of Lee's generals saw this as the best plan. Longstreet, admittedly always looking to turn his corps into an independent command, later recalled that when he rejoined the Army of Northern Virginia after Chancellorsville, 'I proposed to send a force through east Tennessee to join Bragg and also to have Johnston sent to join him, thus concentrating a large force to move against [Union Army of the Tennessee commander William A.] Rosecrans, crush out his army, and march against Cincinnati. That, I thought was the only way we had to relieve Vicksburg.'

Lee disagreed. 'Lee admitted the force of my proposition,' Longstreet recalled, 'but finally stated that he preferred to organise a campaign into Maryland and Pennsylvania, hoping thereby to draw the Federal troops from the southern points they occupied. After discussing the matter with him for several days, I found his mind made up not to allow any of his troops to go west. I then accepted his proposition to make a campaign into Pennsylvania, provided it should be offensive in strategy but defensive in tactics, forcing the Federal army to give us battle when we were in strong position and ready to receive them.'

Lee, always a diplomat, certainly would never have allowed a subordinate to dictate the terms of any of his campaigns or battles, yet gave each of them the impression that he agreed with them. This misunderstanding would later haunt the two of them, during the upcoming campaign and battle at Gettysburg and for years after the war.

On 14 May 1863, Lee went to Richmond and met with Davis and the Secretary of War to discuss future plans. Lee suffered a minor heart attack that spring and would not enjoy perfect health from then on until his death, and this was noted by observers. On 15 May War Department Clerk J. B. Jones noted in his diary, 'Gens. Lee, Stuart, and French were all at the War Department today. Lee looked thinner, and a little pale. Subsequently he and the Secretary of War were long closeted with the President.' Lee remained there, meeting the two officials until the 17th. Although no notes were saved from these meetings, it appears Lee first presented the two with a plan for his army to invade Pennsylvania at that time.

The thought of taking the war north had not just suddenly occurred to Lee. In February 1863 he and Jackson had discussed such a move. In preparation, on 23 February Jackson sent for his chief cartographer, Jedediah Hotchkiss, to draw a map of the Shenandoah Valley all the way north to Harrisburg, the capital of Pennsylvania, and then east to Philadelphia. On 10 March Hotchkiss completed the map and gave it to Jackson who sent it on to Lee. The huge, 32in x 52in map, based on an 1858 map, was detailed to the point of showing residents' names, blacksmiths, mills, and other landmarks. It showed only significant elevations, however, so details in an area such as Gettysburg such as Little Round Top and Seminary Ridge were missing and had to be determined by personal reconnaissance.

On the 18th Lee met Davis and his entire cabinet. Davis was still not positive that Pemberton shouldn't be reinforced rather than Pennsylvania invaded. He was backed by a Texas native, Postmaster General John Reagan. His opinion, stated at the meeting, was that 25–30,000 of Lee's men should be sent to Pemberton. But what of the Shenandoah Valley, he was asked. True, the Valley might fall temporarily, he admitted, but there would still be some 50,000 troops around to defend Richmond.

Lee told the group that he wanted to move north because 'army supplies had become scarce south of that [Potomac] river, while they were abundant north of it'. The invasion plan was further backed by a cabinet member who said that, 'A successful campaign in the territory adjacent to Washington, Baltimore, and Philadelphia might cause the withdrawal of the troops then menacing Vicksburg and Port Hudson.'

'General Grant has reached a position which would prevent dealing with him in that way,' Reagan countered. The destruction of Grant's army would be the only thing to prevent the fall of Vicksburg. Reagan, however, was a lone voice. Even Davis appeared now to back Lee and his plan and Reagan later noted that, 'I could not expect, on such a question, to overrule the opinion of great military men like President Davis and General Lee.' His use of the word 'great' expressed irony, for indeed Davis, a West Point-trained soldier and hero of the Battle of Buena Vista in the Mexican War, saw himself as a military expert. Reagan gave up the attempt. The meeting went on until well after dark and candles were lit in the room, but finally Lee's plan was approved.

Word got around quickly. Jones noted in his diary of 16 May: 'It appears, after the consultation of the generals and the President yesterday, it was resolved not to send [Major General George] Pickett's division to Mississippi, and this morning early the long column marched through the city northward. Gen. Lee is now stronger than he was before the battle [of Chancellorsville] ... There is some purpose on the part of Gen. Lee to have a raid in the enemy's country, surpassing all other raids. If he can organise two columns of cavalry, 5000 each, to move in parallel lines, they may penetrate to the Hudson River; and then the North will discover that it has more to lose by such expeditions than the South. Philadelphia, even, may be taken.' Several days later a fellow government worker offered to bet that 'Gen. Stuart will be in Philadelphia in a fortnight ...'

Longstreet's troops rejoined the army, and Lee returned to his camp and began making preparations for the invasion. He reorganised the Army's two corps that had fought at Chancellorsville earlier, led by Longstreet and Jackson, into three. As he explained in a letter to Davis dated 20 May: 'I have for the past year felt that the corps of this army were too large for one commander ... Each corps contains when in fighting condition about 30,000 men. These are more than one man can properly handle & keep under his eye. They are always beyond the range of his vision, & frequently beyond his reach. The loss of Jackson from the command of one half the army seems to me a good opportunity to remedy this evil ... [Richard Stoddard] Ewell [would receive] ... command of three divisions of Jackson's corps. To take one of Longstreet's divisions [R. H. Anderson's] [and] A. P. Hill's division, & form a division of Ransom's, Cooke's & Pettigrew's brigades, & give the corps thus formed to A. P. Hill. This would make

The extreme left flank position of the Union Army, held by the 20th Maine Infantry, on 2 July. The 15th Alabama attacked up this slope, through these trees, and over these rocks, but were driven back that afternoon.

three corps of three divisions each, under Longstreet, Ewell, and A. P. Hill.' Davis, as usual, bowed to Lee's judgement, and the new arrangement was approved and made.

By June 9 the Federal Bureau of Military Information, part of Hooker's headquarters, had enough details of this new order of battle to describe it with relative accuracy in a report to Hooker.

Within the army, further preparations began. Longstreet's staff officer Moxley Sorrel recalled: 'On the cavalry, special care was bestowed. It had been heavily strengthened and much improved by selections of men and horses. For some time, during inaction, they had been getting good forage and pasturage. Now, when the time was near for the use of this formidable arm under Stuart, its able and famous leader, it was ready for the Commander-in-chief ... The activity of preparation went through all departments – Quartermaster's Subsistence, Ordnance, and Medical. It could be guessed that the military operations would be of great severity and exaction and it behoved all officers of supply to be ready; to fail would be fatal.'

After the successful fight at Chancellorsville, the coffers of ordnance had been filled. Previously the army had suffered by having a number of small 6pdr cannon in its artillery park, weapons incapable of counter-battery fire against superior Union 12- and 10pdrs. Army of Northern Virginia artillery chief Brigadier General William Pendleton wrote home on 26 May: 'I have been exceedingly busy trying to distribute justly, and according to the necessities of the service, the captured guns; also equalising, as far as practicable, the armaments of the several artillery battalions of this army, and securing to the utmost from our means the complete fitness for duty – in the most efficient manner – of all the artillery.'

Cavalry commander Stuart held a review of his three brigades, a total of some 4,000 men, in a broad, open area between Culpeper Court House and Brandy Station. Soon afterwards two more brigades of cavalry arrived to be added to his command, one from the Valley and the other from North Carolina.

With all this work, it's no surprise that word of a potential move by Lee's army reached the excellent intelligence service organised by Hooker's staff almost as soon as preparations were begun. On 22 May a deserter reported that an order from General Lee was read the day before at regimental formations announcing that a movement would soon be made and as a result personal baggage had to be stripped down to the barest minimum. This was confirmed by a spy's report that a Confederate division had recently marched to Culpeper.

Shortly after Lee's men had begun to prepare for the invasion Grant formalised his siege lines around Vicksburg. This called for another meeting on 26 May with Lee and the civilian authorities, this time including the entire Confederate cabinet. Although Davis had been apparently initially convinced of the soundness of Lee's invasion plans, the siege now changed things. The Mississippi native was for detaching troops to send to that state, though the news from Mississippi wasn't all despondent; indeed, much was unrealistically cheerful. Jones noted in his diary on the 25th that the official news was that 'three attempts to carry the city of Vicksburg by assault have been repulsed with heavy loss. Johnston is on the enemy's flank and rear, engendering a new army with rapidity, and if the garrison can hold out a little while, the city may be safe.'

The meeting of the 26th went about the same as that of the 16th. Falsely optimistic news of Johnston's building an army to relieve Vicksburg without the need of Lee's men was discussed. Finally, Lee's plans were approved. As Davis later recalled: 'It was decided by a bold movement to attempt to transfer hostilities to the north side of the Potomac, by crossing the river and marching into Maryland and Pennsylvania, simultaneously driving the foe out of the Shenandoah Valley. Thus, it was hoped, General Hooker's army would be called from Virginia to meet our advance toward the heart of the enemy's country. In that event, the vast preparations which had been made for an advance upon Richmond would be foiled, the plan for his summer's campaign deranged, and much of the season for active operations be consumed in the new combinations and dispositions which would be required. If, beyond the Potomac, some opportunity should be offered so as to enable us to defeat the army on which our foe most relied, the measure of our success would be full; but, if the movement only resulted in freeing Virginia from the presence of the hostile army, it was more than could fairly be expected from awaiting the attack which was clearly indicated.'

Nothing was said about relieving pressure on Vicksburg and Port Hudson in this post-war description of the proposed campaign. Nothing was said about the necessity of getting rations in the North that were unavailable in the South. Nothing was said about Longstreet's clear objective of fighting only a defensive battle. Yet these were clearly objectives in the minds of many when embarking on that campaign.

On the other side of the Rappahannock River, in the Union camp, there was less of a desperate feeling. On the same day as Lee and the Confederate Cabinet were meeting, Army of the Potomac Provost Marshal Marsena Patrick noted in his diary: 'Gen. Hooker left last night for Washington & [Brigadier General Daniel] Butterfield [army chief of staff] has come back, bringing some half a dozen ladies with him, his wife, as I understand, being one of them.'

All the same, Hooker's staff were alert to Lee's activities. Colonel George H. Sharpe, Hooker's intelligence chief, reported on the 27th:

'1. The enemy's line in front of us is much more contracted than during winter. It extends from Banks' ford on a line parallel with the river to near Moss Neck. Anderson's division is on their left. McLaws' is next, and in the rear of Fredericksburg, Early's is massed about Hamilton's Crossing, and Trimble's is directly in the rear of Early. Rhodes' (D. H. Hill's old Divn) is farther to the right, and back from the river, and A. P. Hill's is the right of their line, resting, nearly on Moss Neck. Each of these six division have five brigades.

'2. Pickett's Division of 6 Brigades has come up from Suffolk and is at Taylorsville near Hanover Junction.
'3. Hood's Division of 4 brigades has come up from Suffolk and is between Louisa C. H. and Gordonsville.
'4. Ten days ago there was in Richmond only the City battalion, 2700 strong, commanded by General Elzey.
'5. There are 3 brigades of cavalry 3 miles from Culpeper C. H. towards Kelly's ford. They can at present turn out only 4700 men for duty; but have many dismounted men, and the horses are being constantly and rapidly recruited by the spring growth of grass. These are Fitz Lee's, Wm. H. Fitzhugh Lee's & Wade Hampton's Brigades.
'6. Genl. Jones is still in the Valley, near New Market with about 1400 cavalry & 12 pieces of light Artillery.
'7. Mosby is above Warrenton with 200 men.
'8. The Confed Army is under marching orders and an order from General Lee was very lately read to the troops announcing a campaign of long marches & hard fighting in a part of the country where they would have no railroad transportation.
'9. All the deserters say that the idea is very prevalent in the ranks that they are about to move forward upon or above our right flank.'

Various Confederate commanders also sent out their agents to keep track of the Federals. Longstreet retained a man known as Harrison, said to have been an actor from Richmond, whom he paid in gold for various exploits behind enemy lines. Preparing for the invasion, Longstreet sent for Harrison, telling him to go to Washington to pick up all he could about the Federal army and then meet him at his headquarters in the army (usually close to that of Lee), with this information when possible and worthwhile.

Generally, however, Lee's high command was poorly informed as to the Federal forces and their plans, certainly worse informed than were the Federals. On 30 May Lee wrote to Davis: 'I can get no positive information as to ... [a force said to be gathering on the York River's] strength. I have no knowledge of the scouts sent in that direction. Genl Longstreet, when on the Blackwater, sent a person to Washington. He could get no farther than Baltimore ...'

Lee's new corps commanders began to get their formations into shape and familiarise themselves with their staffs. A. P. Hill took over his command on 6 May; Ewell arrived later, taking command of his corps on 1 June. Late that same day he and the other two corps commanders were summoned to Lee's headquarters where they received their first briefing on the forthcoming campaign. Lee was usually vague in his orders, and his staff let him down by being somewhat amateurish and producing poor marching orders. This had led to disaster in the past, especially in the Seven Days fights around Richmond. This time Lee's orders were detailed only so far as they pertained to the army's movement to Culpeper Court House.

At this meeting Longstreet again proposed a change to his chief's plans. He suggested that the army fight its offensive battle south of the Potomac River, near Culpeper Court House, rather than cross and fight in the north. Longstreet later recalled that he made this suggestion simply 'to bring about a discussion which I thought would give Ewell a better idea of the plan of operations'. Once again, Longstreet showed that he felt he was a better tactician than his commander.

According to Longstreet's later account, Lee generally approved the suggestion – although Lee always seemed agreeable while actually keeping his own counsel. As a result the army was to march slowly and obviously towards Culpeper Court House, forcing Hooker from his strong position on Stafford Heights across the Rappahannock River from Fredericksburg.

The top commanders kept word of Lee's plan to themselves. As late as 10 June, while on the march, Army of Northern Virginia divisional commander Major General Lafayette McLaws wrote home: 'Our destination is not known of course, but circumstances point to a movement towards the valley of the Shenandoah, or towards Pennsylvania. We may go in that direction, or may turn again. So soon as we unloose Hooker from his present base, threatening Richmond. There are many political reasons mixed up with our advance that tis impossible to argue from the mere position our troops are assuming, where our destination will be, or what we are arriving it. If we are striking for Pennsylvania we are actuated by a desire to visit upon the enemy some of the horrors of war, to give the northern people some idea of the excesses committed by their troops upon our houses and inhabitants. On the other hand does it not seem natural to suppose that if we invade their country it will be the means of re-arousing the war spirit which is now apparently fast dying out, and give an excuse for the enforcement of the Conscript act, which the President does not now seem inclined to attempt to put in execution. Thus it appears to many – and it causes much discussion.'

The army's artillery reorganisation was completed on 2 June. Chief of Artillery Pendleton, an Episcopal priest in civilian life and poorly thought of by his much younger subordinates, lost his command of the army artillery reserve, and instead was attached to headquarters almost as an adviser instead of a field commander. The old reserve was broken up and the battalions and batteries assigned to the different corps. While this made for superior fire control and concentration at corps level, it also removed any army-wide ability to concentrate artillery fire under a single command. This lack would be severely felt on the last day of Gettysburg.

Finally, on 3 June, the first of Lee's troops to start north left their old camp grounds. Lafayette McLaws' Division, Longstreet's First Corps, headed towards Culpeper Court House. Hooker, whose administrative abilities led him to create superior intelligence gathering forces, maintained surveillance over the Confederate camps by balloons manned by civilians and soldiers. Because of this, Longstreet headed his men south, out of sight of the balloons, towards

Spotsylvania, only when reaching the wooded area known as the Wilderness turning north-west towards Somerville Ford on the Rapidan. John Bell Hood's division followed, heading for Raccoon Ford.

Ewell's Corps started north the next day, but were stopped when a message arrived from Lee stating that the Federals had laid a pontoon bridge at the mouth of the Deep Run and appeared to be making either a full march or a reconnaissance. Lee wanted Ewell to halt until he could determine which. Going to the front himself, Lee decided it was only a small reconnaissance, and ordered Ewell to continue. A. P. Hill's Corps, Lee decided, was capable of handling the threat.

By 7 June two corps and all his cavalry were at Culpeper Court House. There Stuart staged a grand review of his cavalry. Lee was tied up with more pressing matters and was unable to attend, but Stuart went through with this 8,000-man review that included a massed charge accompanied by blank artillery fire. A gala ball for the officers that evening concluded the festivities. Lee asked to attend a replay on the 8th, and it was arranged for, but according to a report by one of Stuart's staff officers, H. B. McClellan: 'Much less of display was attempted on this occasion, for General Lee, always careful not to tax his men unnecessarily, would not permit the cavalry to take the gallop, nor would he permit the artillerymen to work their guns. He would reserve all their strength for the serious work which must shortly ensue. The movement of his army which resulted in the Gettysburg campaign had commenced ... Longstreet and Ewell had already reached Culpeper Court House, and he wished his cavalry to move across the Rappahannock on the following day, to protect the flank of these corps as they moved northward.'

Army of the Potomac Headquarters was aware that the Confederates were on the move. Signal Corps observers, posted on hills around the Confederate lines, pickets, and balloonists reported abandoned camps and battery positions, dust rising from roads to the west, and nightly rumblings of wagon trains. Hooker wondered if an approach to Richmond were being made along the Peninsula to which Lee was reacting, and wired the commander at Fortress Monroe, John A. Dix, to ask what his men were doing. The reply was negative. Hooker had a reconnaissance made against the Confederate lines at Fredericksburg on 5 June. Prisoners reported that their army's movements were caused by its recent reorganisation. However, news of cavalry reinforcements reaching Stuart's command led to concern that a major raid was in the offing.

Hooker decided to disrupt Confederate plans by making a major attack on Stuart's troops in the early morning of 9 June. General Alfred Pleasonton, a new commander of the Army of the Potomac's cavalry since 22 May, was ordered 'to cross the Rappahannock at Beverly and Kelly's Fords, and march directly on Culpeper ... [and] disperse and destroy the rebel force assembled in the vicinity of Culpeper, and to destroy his trains and supplies of all descriptions to the utmost of your ability ...' To help in this task, Hooker gave Pleasonton two infantry brigades, so the total Union force amounted to some 11,000 men to oppose Stuart's 10,000.

Pleasonton's men left their camp in the afternoon of 8 June, the day that Stuart was holding his grand review for Lee. That evening the Federals reached the fords and camped quietly, without fires, preparing to cross first thing in the morning. They were off a couple of hours before midnight, the lead regiments splashing into the Beverly Ford by four a.m. on the 9th. The division assigned to the crossing at Kelly's Ford, however, did not leave until too late for the rendezvous, and had to make a forced march to catch up with the rest of Pleasonton's men.

While generally the picket reserves in cavalry kept their horses saddled in case of emergency, the Confederate commander square in the way of Pleasonton's advance, had allowed his men to unsaddle their mounts and let them graze reckoning that there was no imminent danger. The Federals, expecting to find their goal at Culpeper Court House rather than Brandy Station, ran right into these troops in the early morning hours, dangerously near where Stuart's artillery had been parked. Half-dressed Confederate cavalrymen, many of them on foot and others bareback, made a fighting retreat until they hit a stone wall at St. James's Episcopal Church. The small, red brick church was two and a quarter miles south-west of Beverly's Ford, at the intersection of Winchester Turnpike and Green's Mill Road. The cemetery lay to the west of the church, between it and the stone wall. Stuart's Horse Artillery unlimbered there, many amidst the tombstones which must have made man-handling the guns into position difficult, and opened fire on the advancing Federals.

The 6th US and 6th Pennsylvania Cavalry charged the Confederate gun line. Confederate artillery commander Major James Hart recalled that they came, '... over a plateau fully eight hundred yards wide, and the objective point was the artillery at the church. Never rode troopers more gallantly than did those steady Regulars, as under a fire of shell and shrapnel, and finally of canister, they dashed up to the very muzzles, then through and beyond our guns, passing between Hampton's left and Jones' right. Here they were simultaneously attacked from both flanks and the survivors driven back.'

Back in Stuart's temporary headquarters at Fleetwood Hill, the sound of artillery woke the Confederate general. Concerned that the Federals might try to cross both Beverly and Kelly's Fords, he sent a brigade to block the road from Kelly's Ford to Brandy Station, while also reinforcing the position at Brandy Station with two more regiments and sending the corps wagon train back to safety in Culpeper.

It was not until eight in the morning that the delayed division crossed Kelly's Ford. Despite the clear sounds of fighting towards Beverly Ford, the commander of this wing of the Federal cavalry sent his lead troops on a road that ran the other way, with no cross-roads until Stevensburg, 4½ miles from the Beverly Ford. In fact he could have gone directly towards the ford or even have taken another road halfway between Kelly's Ford and Stevensburg, a road taken by one Union brigade that led directly to Fleetwood Hill. The odd road choice added an hour to the march required, although, by pure luck, it led troops to avoid running into the brigade that Stuart had stationed on the direct road to Beverly Ford. In fact, that brigade saw very little fighting at all that day, for despite his receiving word that the Federals eventually were moving beyond his right flank to Beverly Ford, the brigade commander, Beverly Robertson, made no move to counter this march.

Instead, Robertson allowed his force to be essentially pinned down by a single Federal unit that approached, but did not attack, his position. Stuart reported that Robertson, 'did not conform to the movement of the enemy to the right, of which he was cognisant, so as to hold him on check or thwart him by a corresponding move of a portion of his command in the same direction ...' Although he did not remove Robertson from command, he lost any trust in this subordinate and left his command with Lee's main army while he moved into Maryland and Pennsylvania later. This would have severe consequences for Lee's entire campaign.

By late morning Federals reached the base of Fleetwood Hill. Stuart had to hold this hill or his troops at St. James's Church would be cut off. The only Confederates on the hill at the moment were the crew of a 6pdr cannon that had fired off all its ammunition except some round shot during the battle around the church and was being withdrawn to replenish the limber chest. The staff officer whom Stuart had left on the hill sent hurried news to Stuart of the fight at St. James's Church, while ordering the cannon to open up with its round shot. Stuart dashed a couple of regiments back and they reached the hill just as the cannon, having fired its last round, was limbering up and being withdrawn and the Federals were advancing.

Attack and counter-attack swept over the hill, with one side or the other in control of it at various times. Exhausted men and horses fell. One squadron of the 1st New Jersey found that 27 men had had their horses killed or wounded under them so that there were left 'not a dozen horses that could charge – not a man who could shout above a whisper'. In the end, the last of the Federals were forced off the hill and Stuart's rear was safe. He set up a new, formidable line of battle based on Fleetwood Hill. Confederate infantry, having been sent towards the sound of the guns, arrived on the field, but by that time the Federals had begun to retreat towards the fords.

On paper, the affair was a clear Confederate victory. They had suffered only 10 per cent losses, with not a man down in Robertson's missing brigade. The Federal troops had failed to destroy or even disrupt Stuart's cavalry. In fact, although they had learned that there were infantry near the cavalry, they were unable to take any prisoners or even provide their headquarters with any accurate details as to the enemy's formations. Even so, the Battle at Brandy Station was to have a profound effect on the Gettysburg Campaign. Where in the past Confederate cavalry seemed invincible, it now seemed flawed. It was widely admitted that Stuart's cavalry had been surprised, that their guard had been let down. When coupled with the widely discussed review held earlier, Stuart appeared to be more of a parade ground soldier than a true warrior. A writer in the Richmond *Examiner* noted: 'The more the circumstances of the late affair at Brandy Station are considered, the less pleasant do they appear. If this was an isolated case it might be excused under the convenient head of an accident or chance; but this much puffed cavalry of Northern Virginia has been twice, if not three times, surprised since the battles of last December and such repeated accidents can be regarded as nothing but necessary consequences of negligence and bad management. If the war was a tournament invented and supported for the pleasure and profit of a few vain and weak-headed officers, these disasters might be dismissed with compassion. But the country pays dearly for the blunders which encourage the enemy to overrun and devastate the land with cavalry which is daily learning to despise the mounted troops of the Confederacy. It is high time that this branch of the service be reformed.'

Stuart was deeply mortified. As vain and ambitious as any Civil War officer ever was, he felt that his good name must be restored by a repeat of some of the type of raids that had gained him fame originally, such as his command's ride around McClellan's army during the Peninsula Campaign. So Lee would start off on this campaign with an artillery chief who essentially had no command duties and whom few of his subordinates trusted; a cavalry commander who was out to prove himself; one corps commander who had shown that he would not immediately hop to any of Lee's orders without discussing his own ideas first; and two corps commanders who were brand-new to their commands. From a command point of view, Lee's was a most difficult position indeed.

At the same time, the Union cavalry, who had felt bested by their Confederate counterparts time and again, gained tremendously in morale after Brandy Station. A soldier in the 1st Maine Cavalry noted that after the fight his regiment, 'became self-reliant and began to comprehend its own possibilities. It became inspired with an invincible spirit that never again forsook it. These remarks might be extended ... to our cavalry generally.'

Pleasonton's raid did cause Lee to wait a day to see if it was to be followed up. When it appeared not, he sent word to Ewell, heading towards Chester's Gap that led the way into the Shenandoah Valley towards Winchester, to resume his advance. By the morning of 12 June Ewell's lead elements were through the gap and had reached Front Royal in the Valley itself. On the previous day the Federal commander in the Valley, Robert Milroy, had received orders from Washington to, 'immediately take steps to remove your command from Winchester to Harpers Ferry'. No mention was made of Ewell's approach, however, and an innocent Milroy protested that he was strong enough at Winchester to defend his post there.

Nevertheless on the 12th Milroy sent out reconnaissance parties who soon ran into large groups of infantry, cavalry, and artillery and reported the fact to Milroy. He chose not to believe them, explaining to Washington that, 'Officers of my command and reliable scouts who were present gave contradictory reports.'

On the morning of 13 June Ewell's men made contact with Milroy's defences. The Confederates advanced and the Federals fought well, but flanked at point to point, by dusk had to fall back north of a line formed by Abram's Creek and the mill race. By now Milroy had learned from prisoners that he was being confronted by Ewell's entire corps. The proper move would have been to escape north, something he could have done that night. Instead, he telegraphed to Washington that, 'I can hold this place five days if you can relieve me in that time. They will surround, but can't take my fortification.'

The next day Ewell moved on Milroy's flanks and front. Suddenly deciding he was short of rations and ammunition, Milroy ordered an evacuation, and his troops began to move north early in the morning of 15 June. The Confederates, however, had anticipated this, and completely surrounded the Federal force. While some managed to fight their way out of the trap, the Confederates in the end bagged almost half of Milroy's division, some 3,000 officers and men, and effectively destroyed that organisation as a combat force. Ewell had exceeded Lee's fondest hopes.

As Ewell was bagging Milroy, Hooker began to move. He detached a wing of the army under I Corps commander John Reynolds north towards Manassas, with the rest of the army following. Left behind was his group of balloonists and their equipment, after the army's chief signals officer had declined responsibility for the band, a number of personal disputes, and the general difficulty in using and caring for the equipment. It would be missed. Hooker's army was not in great spirits; 'We are likely to be outgeneralled & for ought I know, whipped out again by Lee, at Manassas,' noted the army's provost marshal, Marsena Patrick, on 13 June. In fact, when Hooker reached Manassas from his base in Fairfax on the 15th Lee was still missing, and Hooker slowly advanced his men so that by

A period photograph of the spot where Major General Reynolds was mortally wounded, the exact spot being pointed out by a Gettysburg inhabitant. Union skirmishers were in line in the cornfield in the distance when Reynolds was shot. (*Photographic History of the Civil War*)

the 21st he had two divisions of II Corps, led by William Scott Hancock, at Thoroughfare Gap; V Corps, led by George Gordon Meade, near Aldie Gap; and XII Corps, under Henry Slocum, at Leesburg. All were in position to block any attempt by Lee to turn east and drive on Washington. Slocum got permission to lay pontoon bridges across the Potomac, so that by 25 June a way for the entire army to move north easily was available.

On 16 June, Hill's Corps, the last of Lee's infantry to move north, began to pull out of Fredericksburg, and one of Ewell's divisions reached the Potomac River at Shepherdstown from Winchester, following several other Confederate units already across that river. Hooker was still not sure of what Lee was up to. Patrick, not a Hooker admirer, noted in his diary on 17 June that Hooker 'acts like a man without a plan and is entirely at a loss what to do, or how to match the enemy, or counteract his movements ...'

On 23 June Hooker made a quick trip to Washington to meet President Abraham Lincoln, Secretary of War Edwin Stanton, and the Army's General-in-Chief, Major General Henry Halleck. What was discussed is not known, although it appears that there was a debate about holding Harpers Ferry (Hooker against, and Halleck for, with Lincoln agreeing with Halleck). Whatever happened, it was widely reported that he was drunk when he returned to the army on the 24th.

Meanwhile Stuart's cavalry was covering the Confederate right. Its job was to keep Federal cavalry from discovering the exact location or strength of the Confederate main forces. On the 16th his men splashed across the Rappahannock, heading towards the Bull Run/Catoctin Mountains and Blue Ridge, leaving some troops near the Rappahannock to screen the infantry until the last of the army had passed. On the 17th Confederate cavalry clashed with Federal cavalry under young General Judson Kilpatrick. As at Brandy Station, neither side won a clear victory, and the Confederates fell back towards Middleburg to await further orders.

In the evening of the 17th Confederates attacked a lone Federal cavalry regiment in Middleburg, driving them out and taking a number of prisoners. Stuart gathered his men in Middleburg on the 18th and was attacked there the next day by a full division of Federal cavalry. Eventually the Confederates were forced back, but still managed to place themselves between the Federals and Lee's infantry. But Pleasonton's suddenly aggressive cavalry would not leave the Southern mounted men alone. He attacked again on 21 June and again forced the Confederates to withdraw from the area around Upperville. For the first time ever, Stuart's Horse Artillery lost a gun to Federal cavalry during the action. Indeed, concerned about the outcome of the battle, Lee actually sent McLaws' division to Ashby's Gap in case of an emergency, something that could not have pleased the proud Stuart.

Yet the Confederate cavalry was doing a good job of screening Lee's advance and now Stuart wrote for further orders. Lee wrote back that if he felt that he could hold the gaps in the Blue Ridge with two brigades, he could move north along with Ewell's Corps with the rest of his forces. Longstreet, to whom Stuart also wrote, felt that Stuart could pass by the rear of the Army of the Potomac to cross the Potomac and head north, adding that Lee agreed with this move. Intelligence from partisan ranger commander John S. Mosby, whose unit had been active in this area, indicated that this was indeed possible.

On 22 June Lee sent further orders to his subordinates that would dictate their immediate future moves. He told Ewell to send two divisions and a brigade of cavalry towards the Susquehanna River, some to pass through Emmitsburg, Maryland, others through Chambersburg, Pennsylvania, and the rest through McConnellsburg, Pennsylvania. If Harrisburg were to come within his 'means', Ewell was to capture that city as well. But his main task was to gather supplies, especially food. In fact, Ewell would be so successful in this that between 10 and 29 June his forces confiscated 3,000 cattle and 5,000 barrels of flour, amounting to some 980,000 pounds, paying for it with Confederate paper money, which was worthless in the North. The flour captures alone would be enough to feed the whole of Lee's army a full daily ration for thirteen days.

In pouring rain in the evening of 23 June, Stuart's adjutant received a long message from Lee that he passed on to his general. According to the adjutant, H. B. McClellan, 'It informed General Stuart that General Early would move upon York, Pa., and that he was desired to place his cavalry as speedily as possible with that, the advance division of Lee's right wing'. The letter suggested that, as the roads leading northward from Shepherdstown and Williamsport were already encumbered by the infantry, the artillery, and the transportation of the army, the delay which would necessarily occur in passing by these would, perhaps, be greater than would ensue if General Stuart passed around the enemy's rear. The letter further informed him that, if he chose the latter route, General Early would receive instructions to look out for him and endeavor to communicate with him; and York, Pa., was designated as the point in the vicinity of which he was to expect to hear from Early, and as the possible (if not the probable) point of concentration of the army.' If, however, the Army of the Potomac were to remain where it was, thereby threatening Richmond, Stuart was to withdraw west of the Blue Ridge, then cross at Shepherdstown and move to Frederick, Maryland, where he would threaten Washington, a short distance east.

Once again poor staff work and a general behavioural pattern of Lee to make his orders somewhat vague, giving wide discretion to the recipient would lead to a major problem. In this case, Stuart, smarting from his scrapes at Brandy Station and Middleburg, wanted to do something spectacular to retrieve his waning public reputation. Taking the route that Mosby suggested offered a chance to destroy much of the wagon train of the Army of the Potomac, cut communications between Hooker and Pleasonton, damage the Chesapeake and Ohio Canal and Baltimore & Ohio Railroad, and create a sensation in Washington. While Lee appears to have expected Stuart to stay close to Ewell, since he believed that

Hooker would follow him north, Stuart decided to do this latter move instead. The two brigades he left with Lee guarding the passes were those commanded by Robertson, who had performed poorly at Brandy Station, and 'Grumble' Jones, with whom he did not get along.

At any rate Lee now made known down to lower command levels that his plan was to invade Pennsylvania. Word of this impending Confederate invasion reached Pennsylvania where it caused quite a stir. On 16 June Philadelphia lawyer Sidney George Fisher noted in his diary: 'The news is that the rebels have entered Penna: in large force & have taken Chambersburg. They are said to have 18,000 men. Went to town ... The streets were crowded, the State House bell was tolling to call the people together to enroll for the defense of the state. Telegrams came from the governor [Andrew Curtin] urging strenuous efforts to send men forward to Harrisburg, which the rebels, after taking Carlisle, were rapidly approaching.' On 15 June the US government called for 100,000 volunteer militia to defend the state, with Pennsylvania supplying half the troops. The response, however, especially along the Maryland border, was poor. Many of the farmers there were of German origin and had no particular interest in the war; indeed, many were even pro-Southern. Many were members of the Amish and Mennonite pacifist sects and therefore felt neutral. Arthur Fremantle, a British observer with Lee's army, noted that the 'Pennsylvania Dutch ... are the most unpatriotic people I ever saw, and openly state that they don't care which side wins, provided they are left alone'.

The response to Curtin's call was poor, although some militia units, many reformed from three-month regiments released after Chancellorsville, did come forward. Other civilians chose to pack up as much as they could and head north, east, or west to perceived safety. The state government packed up its records and sent them away as well.

Pennsylvania was part of a new army department, commanded by Major General Darius Couch. He had performed excellently at Chancellorsville, where his cool behaviour as commander after Hooker's removal from the field helped prevent disaster. Offered command of the Army of the Potomac, ill health forced his refusal and he ended up in this backwater instead. He would prove helpful not in the final battle of the campaign, but in preparing and forwarding local militia units as they gathered in Harrisburg to threatened sites so that the main Army of the Potomac need not try to defend every post in the state.

From 22 to 25 June, during which time it rained heavily, Longstreet and Hill's Corps arrived at and crossed the Potomac River. Sergeant J. Warren Stark, 7th Louisiana, wrote to his brother later: 'Arrived at Shepherdstown on [the] 19th & found the river so high that we could not cross so we lay by until the 22nd. Then waded across, the water was waist deep & quite swift. I fell twice in crossing and of course got wet.'

At the Army of the Potomac headquarters, Hooker, not knowing of the final Confederate crossing, prepared to move, writing to Washington on 24 June that

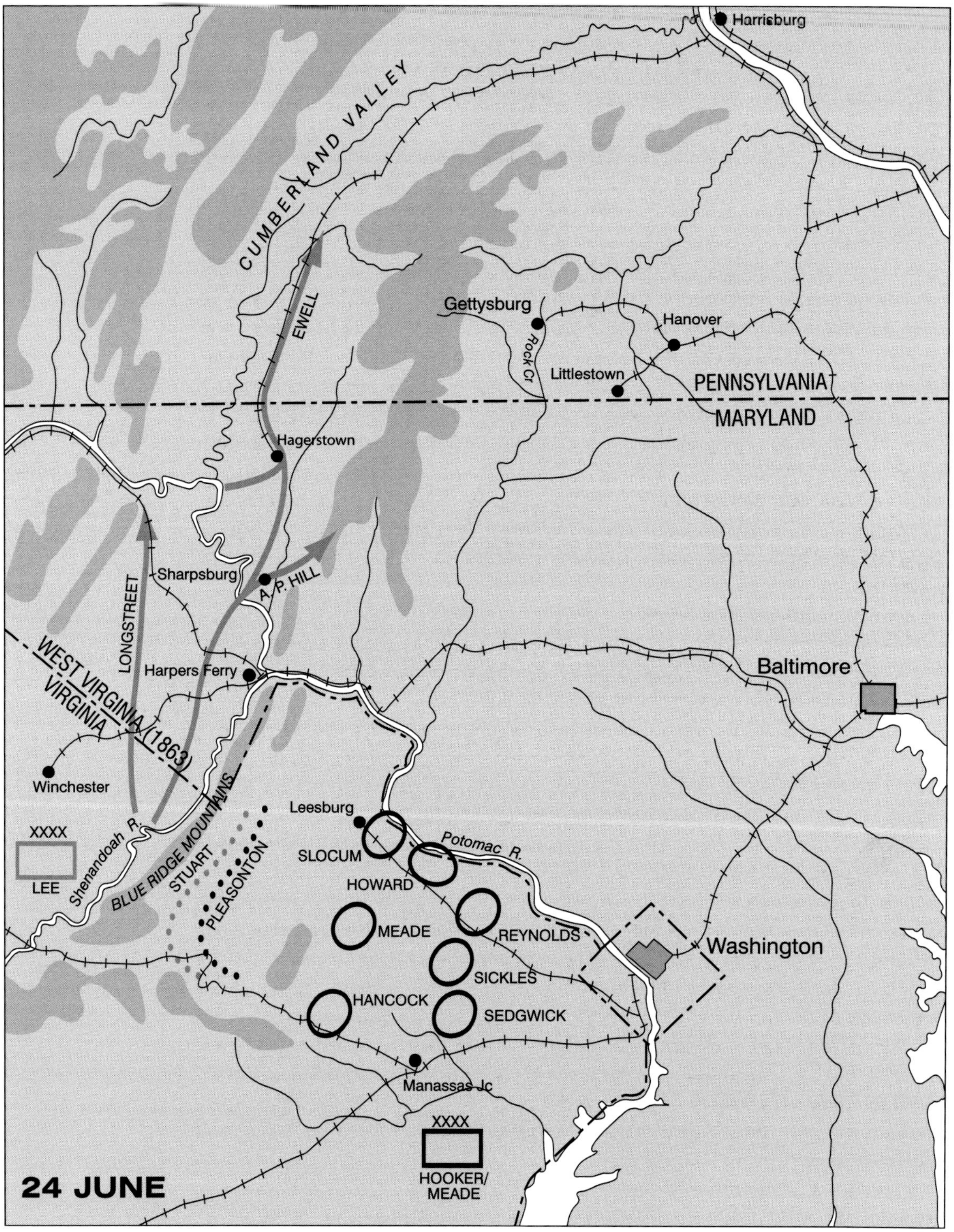
Harrisburg
CUMBERLAND VALLEY
EWELL
Gettysburg
Rock Cr
Hanover
Littlestown
PENNSYLVANIA
MARYLAND
Hagerstown
Sharpsburg
A. P. HILL
LONGSTREET
WEST VIRGINIA (1863)
VIRGINIA
Harpers Ferry
Baltimore
Winchester
Leesburg
Potomac R.
XXXX
LEE
Shenandoah R.
BLUE RIDGE MOUNTAINS
STUART
PLEASONTON
SLOCUM
HOWARD
MEADE
REYNOLDS
Washington
SICKLES
HANCOCK
SEDGWICK
Manassas Jc
XXXX
HOOKER/
MEADE
24 JUNE

he was going to send two corps across the river to cut off Ewell 'from the balance of the rebel army, in case he should make a protracted sojourn with his Pennsylvania neighbors', while striking the Confederate line of communications to Richmond with the rest of the army. These plans were spoiled, however, by word received that day from one of the army's most trusted scouts, 'I learn beyond a doubt that the last of Lee's entire army has passed through Martinsburg towards the Potomac.' Hooker now had to cross the river with his entire army. His infantry had all crossed the Potomac by the 26th, the cavalry following the next day. By midnight of the 27th, all the troops having crossed, engineers removed the bridges and followed the army.

Hooker's men concentrated around Frederick, and the general telegraphed Washington for reinforcements, saying, like McClellan before him on the Peninsula, that the enemy outnumbered him and he was unable to attack. Being refused these, he asked again to be allowed to abandon Harpers Ferry. Halleck said no, and with that Hooker telegraphed his resignation to Halleck. Lincoln, who had lost trust in his general, accepted it, telling his cabinet on 28 June that Hooker had been relieved. His replacement would be V Corps Commander Major General George Gordon Meade. The choice had been made by Lincoln and Stanton, in a late night conference at the War Department, without any input from Halleck. The luckless Army of the Potomac would have its fifth commander in two years.

Stuart's Confederate cavalry didn't get moving until the early morning hours of 25 June, having first had to send back his wagons, ambulances, and all but six pieces of artillery. Almost right away he ran into the Army of the Potomac's II Corps, and was forced to retire to make his detour, having no intention of abandoning his move around the entire Federal army because of this setback. On the 27th his troops reached Wolf Run Shoals on the Occoquan River, crossing the next day to Fairfax Station and, from there, on to the Potomac at Rowser's Ford. As the infantry had discovered farther upstream, the Potomac was swollen by recent rains. It took him until three the next morning to get his men, horses, and guns across into Maryland.

Once there he learned from prisoners that the Army of the Potomac was on the march to Frederick, with Hooker's headquarters being located at Poolesville. Deciding it was more important than ever to reach Ewell, he pushed forward on the 28th. Entering the town of Rockville, Maryland, not far from Washington, Stuart's troopers ran into a 150-strong Federal wagon train bound for the Army of the Potomac. As the wagonners and their escorts tried to escape, the grey troopers swarmed around them. Some Federals wrecked their wagons and mounted the horses to escape more quickly and some wagons did get away, but Stuart's men suddenly found themselves in possession of 125 wagons filled with grain for horses, food and whiskey, and 400 prisoners.

Stuart's men spent the rest of the 28th and well into the night parolling prisoners, feeding their tired horses and themselves. It would not be until 29 June

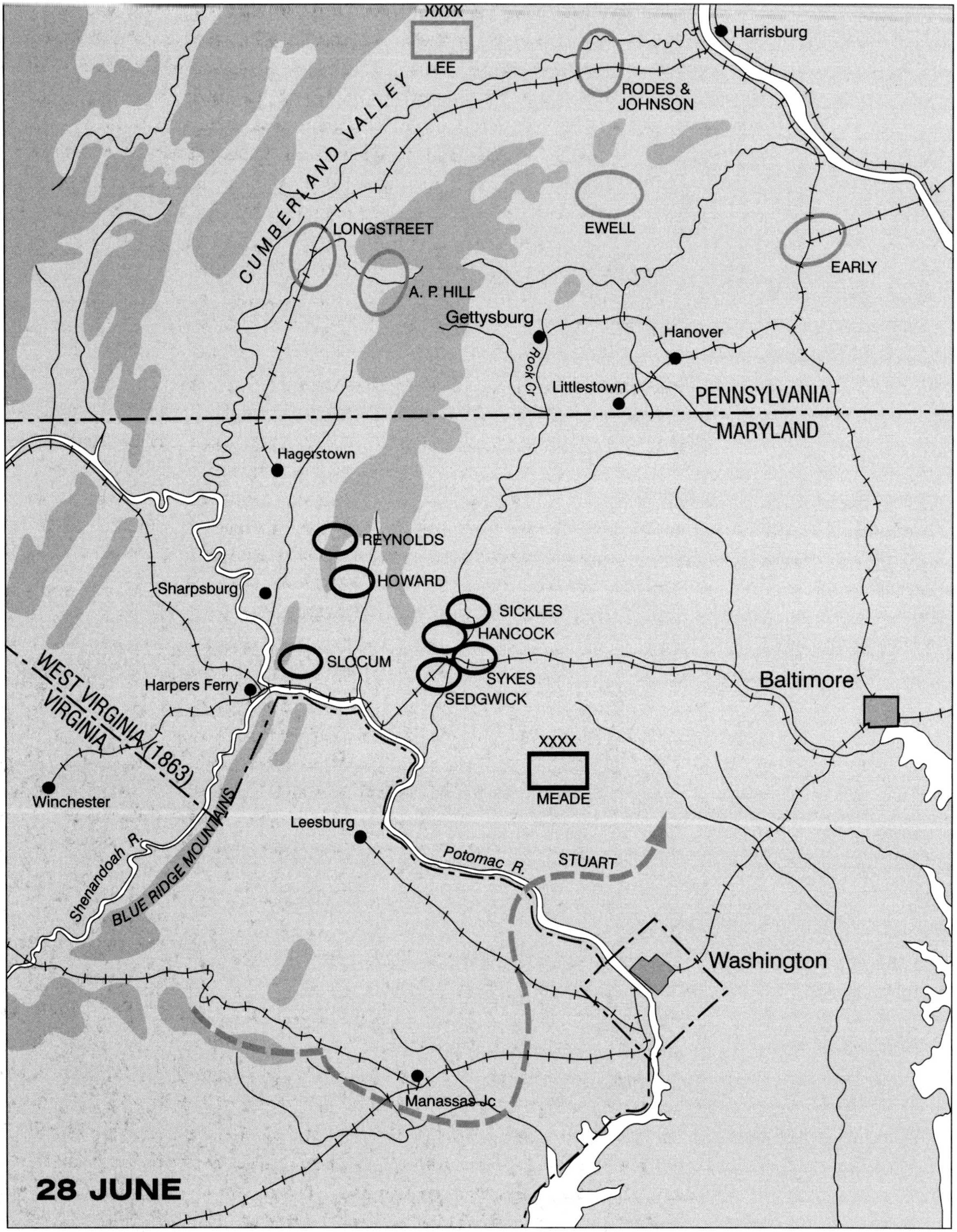
XXXX
LEE
Harrisburg
RODES &
JOHNSON
CUMBERLAND VALLEY
EWELL
LONGSTREET
EARLY
A. P. HILL
Gettysburg
Hanover
Rock Cr.
Littlestown
PENNSYLVANIA
MARYLAND
Hagerstown
REYNOLDS
HOWARD
Sharpsburg
SICKLES
HANCOCK
SLOCUM
SYKES
SEDGWICK
Harpers Ferry
Baltimore
WEST VIRGINIA
VIRGINIA
(1863)
XXXX
MEADE
Winchester
Leesburg
Potomac R.
STUART
Shenandoah R.
BLUE RIDGE MOUNTAINS
Washington
Manassas Jc
28 JUNE

that Stuart again took to the road, and this time he was burdened by the wagons that he insisted must be brought to the main Confederate army. This would slow him down greatly so that he would not be able to perform his most important function, that of screening Ewell's corps in the advance of the army, quickly.

In the meantime Lee was unaware that Hooker had brought the Federal army across the river two days earlier. He would not learn of this until the 28th and it would not be from the source he expected, Stuart's cavalry. On that day he sent out orders to his corps commanders for an advance on Harrisburg. Ewell's column had gone via Chambersburg to Carlisle, while others had gone east as far as the Susquehanna River at Wrightsville which they had reached by 27 June. There they found a wooden bridge set afire by local militia, and, unable to cross the wide river into Lancaster County, retired to York, where they bivouacked on the night of the 28th.

The 28th was Meade's first full day of command, and he picked a conservative but reasonable strategy. He would set up a line of defences along Pipe Creek, Maryland, just below the Pennsylvania line. His reasoning was that Lee, learning of the Army of the Potomac's presence in Maryland so near elements of the Army of Northern Virginia, would concentrate his forces for an attack. The area he picked was an excellent defensive line, with 1,000- to 800-foot high ridges as much as four to ten miles deep. Most elevations in the area are only 400 to 500 feet high, so this was a highly defendable position.

In the meantime Lee's troops spread out, gathering supplies. Looting was strictly forbidden, and this order was taken seriously. On the eve of the battle a visiting Austrian officer, Fitzgerald Ross, noted seeing the Army of Northern Virginia's Inspector General, 'Riding about seeking whom he could devour in the shape of a depredator or illegal annexer of private property; but I do not think he found any. Indeed, the good behaviour and discipline of the men of this army is surprising to me, considering the way in which the Northerners have devastated the country and wreaked their wrath on women and children in the South wherever they had an opportunity.' Confederates did not even burn the buildings at Carlisle that housed the Regular US Army's cavalry training centre, although they did set fire to the Caledonia Iron Works, which belonged to Radical Republican Representative Thaddeus H. Stevens. At points they were met by Pennsylvania Emergency Militia troops, who offered virtually no resistance, being 'raw and undisciplined', as well as untrained.

Passing through Gettysburg, where they found supplies of shoes and hats, Early's Division of Ewell's Corps gathered more hats, shoes, and socks, as well as beef cattle, paying for the latter in US currency which the unit had requisitioned from towns in its path: at York 27–28 June and at Carlisle on the 28th (medicine, arms, saddlery and provisions). A. P. Hill's Corps, led by Henry Heth's Division, entered Chambersburg on the 26th. Longstreet's Corps, except Pickett's Division which had been left behind, moved to Greenwood on the Gettysburg Pike on 29 June. Lee set up headquarters near Chambersburg, remaining there until the

30th. In all, it is estimated that prior to 1 July the Confederates, during this invasion, had gathered 916 pigs, 4,228 beef cattle, 1,023 cows, 6,762 barrels of flour, 7,901 bushels of wheat, 2,399 sheep (badly needed to produce wool uniforms in the South), 28,855 pounds of bacon, and 22,544 pounds of other meat. Also, many northern horses appeared in the Confederate ranks, and these were not always formally requisitioned or paid for.

On 28 June the stage was set for the eventual battle. Stuart found out that the Union army was across the Potomac, moving on Frederick. He belatedly realised that is was vital that he join Lee's troops, 'with', he reported later, 'as little delay as possible ... [so that] he could acquaint the commanding general with the nature of the enemy's movements'. He decided to head up through Hanover to join Lee's main force, but instead found Federal cavalry in the town. There the Confederate troopers were badly handled, and Stuart, still burdened with his captured wagons, was forced to make a detour, not reaching Carlisle, where he hoped to meet Confederate infantry, until 1 July, too late to provide Lee with information about the Federals' approach.

Longstreet's spy Harrison arrived at his general's headquarters that evening with the information that three Federal corps were near Frederick, and two more were near the base of South Mountain. Two more were missing, but those accounted for more than equalled the Confederate Army in terms of numbers. This information was quickly brought to Lee who reacted swiftly, ordering his far-flung troops to march towards Cashtown where he would concentrate his army. Their march began on 29 June. That day, he ordered Ewell's Corps to concentrate at Heidlersburg, ten miles north of Gettysburg, from where he could either go to Cashtown or move into Gettysburg. On the 30th Ewell, learning that Hill's Corps was at Cashtown, sent his troops to join him. To avoid bottlenecks on the narrow dirt roads, he sent some troops direct and others through Hunterstown, near Gettysburg. This column commander was given permission to go through Gettysburg if 'circumstances dictate'. On the evening of 29 June citizens in Gettysburg could see the campfires of Ewell's leading division, that led by Henry Heth, outside their town.

At the same time, Meade, whose vague intelligence suggested that the Confederate Army was or would shortly be in Harrisburg, ordered his corps north. The I and XI Corps were to move on Emmitsburg, Maryland; the III and XII Corps were directed to Taneytown; the II Corps was to move on Frizzleberg; the V Corps, to Union; and the VI Corps, to Windsor. Still hoping to fight along Pipe Creek, on the 30th Meade ordered VI Corps, on the army's right, to Manchester, in the rear of Pipe Creek; II Corps together with Meade's headquarters, were to go to Taneytown; the XII and V Corps, in the army's centre, were to deploy around Two Taverns and Hanover, just in front of Pipe Creek; the I, III, and XI Corps, forming the army's left flank, would go to the cross-roads town of Gettysburg.

The stage was set for a major collision.

2

ARMIES AND LEADERS

LEADERS OF THE ARMY OF THE POTOMAC

George Gordon Meade

Commander of the Army of the Potomac. Born in Spain on 31 December 1815 to a wealthy family that lost its money through loyalty to the Napoleonic cause during the Peninsular War, he was sent to Mount Hope Institution, Baltimore, Maryland, before entering the US Military Academy at West Point. He graduated 19th in the 56-strong Class of 1834. After only short service in Florida, he resigned from the army in 1836 to take up civil engineering. In 1842 he returned to the army as a lieutenant in the Corps of Topographical Engineers, seeing service in the Mexican War where he was brevetted first lieutenant.

At the outbreak of the Civil War Meade was a captain, but Pennsylvania's Governor Andrew Curtin had him appointed a brigadier general of volunteers. He led a brigade of Pennsylvania troops in the Peninsula Campaign where he was badly wounded at the Battle of Glendale. He had not fully recovered when he resumed command for service at the Second Manassas. For his service, he was given divisional command, leading his troops at South Mountain, Antietam, and Fredericksburg. His division in I Corps was one of the only Union units on the field at Fredericksburg to see any success, and thereafter he was given command of V Corps. He commanded this corps at Chancellorsville.

After the resignation of Joseph Hooker as Army of the Potomac commander, President Lincoln first asked Major General Darius Couch, who commanded at Chancellorsville when Hooker had to leave the field, to take command. Couch, however, pleaded poor health and recommended Meade for the job. Quite to his surprise, Meade was given army command on 28 June 1863.

Meade, therefore, was new to overall command. While he knew his corps commanders socially and profession-

Major General George Gordon Meade. (*Military Images* Magazine)

ally, he had never commanded them and had no specific knowledge of their corps' capabilities and problems. Nor was he close to other important Union officers in the field, such as his artillery commander, Henry Hunt. He was not well acquainted with his commander-in-chief, Abraham Lincoln, the Secretary of War, Edwin Stanton, or the army's general-in-chief, Henry Halleck. Finally, he was not well known by most of the army. His own Pennsylvania troops thought well of him, and this reputation spread by rumour throughout the ranks. Most other troops adopted a 'wait and see' attitude. Meade was aware that until now command of the Army of the Potomac was a revolving door, unsuccessful generals being booted out without ceremony. His job of learning about and organising an army already on the march in potentially the most important campaign of its life, one on its own soil, would be quite difficult. He was bound to be cautious.

Lee, on learning of Meade's appointment, noted that he would 'commit no blunder on my front and if I make one he will make haste to take advantage of it'.

Although his troops admired him, Meade was a difficult man to like personally. He was most notable for his quick temper, often chewing out subordinates unfairly and without knowing all the circumstances. Subordinates dreaded bringing him bad news, knowing that they would bear the brunt of his reaction.

Staff officer Frank Haskell described Meade as 'a tall spare man, with full beard, which with his hair, originally brown, is quite thickly sprinkled with gray – has a Romanish face, very large nose, and a white, large forehead, prominent and wide over the eyes, which are full and large, and quick in their movements, and he wears spectacles ... His habitual personal appearance is quite careless, and it would be rather difficult to make him look well dressed.'

John Fulton Reynolds I Corps Commander. Born in Lancaster, Pennsylvania, only a day's trip from Gettysburg, on 20 September 1820, he attended local schools before entering the US Military Academy. A graduate in the Class of 1841, he was assigned to the artillery where he earned brevet promotions to the rank of major during the Mexican War. In September 1860 he was named Commandant of Cadets at West Point, where he also was an instructor of tactics.

On the war's outbreak he was appointed lieutenant colonel of the 14th US Infantry Regiment, and was then appointed brigadier general of volunteers on 26 August 1861. Captured during the Peninsula Campaign in June 1862 while in command of a brigade, he was exchanged that August and given command of the 3rd Division, III Corps, for the Second Manassas. He commanded Pennsylvania Militia called up for the Antietam Campaign, and then returned to the army as commander of I Corps, in which Meade's division served at Fredericksburg. He had been named major general of volunteers on 29 November 1862.

After Chancellorsville it was widely rumoured that he had been offered command of the Army of the Potomac but declined it because of controls he felt would have been imposed by the administration in Washington. At any rate, when his earlier subordinate Meade was named to the post, one of the first things Meade did was to call for Reynolds. Greeting him warmly outside his tent, the two talked about what to do in the present emergency. Meade gave Reynolds command of the left wing of the army, which was then moving after Lee, who accepted it without any complaint about serving under Meade. In fact, Reynolds told Meade at their meeting that he would have been obliged to accept the command had it come to him, 'but I am glad it did not'.

Major General John F. Reynolds. This woodcut of him appeared with his obituary in the 18 July 1863 issue of *Harper's Weekly*.

Riding into Gettysburg on 1 July after receiving an urgent summons from cavalry outside the town, Reynolds began organising a defence there. He placed the three corps under his command into position, and, while leading the 2nd Wisconsin Infantry forward, was shot and killed. His body was taken to Lancaster where he was buried in the town cemetery three days later. His was an important loss to the Union troops, as he inspired confidence in his men and was a superior corps commander. His command was taken over by Abner Doubleday.

Staff officer Haskell recalled that Reynolds 'was the very beau ideal of the gallant general. Mounted upon a superb black horse, with his head thrown back and his great black eyes flashing fire, he was everywhere upon the field, seeing all things and giving commands in person.'

John Newton

I Corps Commander. As senior divisional commander in I Corps on 1 July 1863, Abner Doubleday assumed corps command on Reynolds' death. Meade, however, felt that Doubleday was too slow and pedantic for the job. He selected a divisional commander from VI Corps, John Newton, to replace Reynolds, even though Doubleday had seniority. Hence, John Newton commanded I Corps for the remainder of Gettysburg.

Newton was a Virginia native, born in Norfolk on 25 August 1822. Graduating second in the US Military Academy Class of 1842, the same class as Doubleday, he went into the Corps of Engineers, in which he served until the Civil War. On 23 September 1861, he was named a brigadier general of volunteers, finally taking a field command for the first time in his military career during the Peninsula Campaign. After Antietam he was promoted to divisional command. He performed well in combat in all his actions through Chancellorsville, in which his division took Marye's Heights over Fredericksburg. Despite having written directly to Lincoln with complaints about Army of the Potomac Commander Ambrose Burnside after the December 1862 Battle of Fredericksburg, he was promoted to major general of volunteers 30 March 1863.

Staff officer Haskell wrote: 'Newton is a well-sized, shapely, muscular, well-dressed man, with brown hair, with a very ruddy, clean-shaved, full face, blue eyes, blunt, round features, walks very erect, curbs in his chin, and has somewhat of that smart sort of swagger that people are apt to suppose characterises soldiers.'

Winfield Scott Hancock II Corps Commander. Another Pennsylvanian, he was born on 14 February 1824 outside Norristown, where he was schooled until attending the US Military Academy. He was graduated 18th out of 25 cadets in the Class of 1844, apparently the youngest cadet in that class. He earned a brevet in the Mexican War, seeing action thereafter in the Kansas War and in the expedition into Utah to oppose the Mormons. At the outbreak of the Civil War he was serving as chief quartermaster in Los Angeles, California. He made his way east to be appointed brigadier general of volunteers, ranking from 23 September 1861. He commanded a brigade in the 1862 campaigns, rising to command a division of II Corps at Antietam when its previous commander was mortally wounded. He was given the rank of major general of volunteers to date from 29 November 1862. At Fredericksburg his command served well, and he covered the retreat of his division at Chancellorsville, essentially covering the army's retreat.

When he arrived on the field at Gettysburg, he found Reynolds dead and the Federal forces there driven through the town. He immediately assumed command of the entire field, despite objections from Oliver O. Howard, who out ranked him on the army list. Hancock confirmed Howard's decision to fight on Cemetery Hill, strengthening his lines there.

When Meade arrived that night, Hancock led his generals in arguing to fight there, rather than fall back to the Pipe Creek position that Meade favoured. His point of view won over, and his hard fighting on 2 and 3 July in the centre and on the right of the Union line helped win the battle to a great extent. However, there was a problem when Hancock ordered cannon near the objective of Pickett's Charge to reopen fire after artillery commander Henry Hunt ordered them stilled to preserve ammunition. Hancock was correct in worrying that their silence would badly affect his infantry's morale, but wrong since it was not his position to assume command of artillery in his area and his orders caused a shortage of long-range ammunition when the Confederate infantry did finally emerge to begin their assault.

Major General Winfield Scott Hancock. (*Military Images* Magazine)

During that assault Hancock's saddle was hit by a bullet that drove bits of wood and a nail into his thigh. He remained on the field long enough to see the attack stopped before being taken to a field hospital.

Staff officer Haskell thought Hancock was 'the tallest and most shapely, and in many respects the best looking [general] officer of them all. His hair is very light brown, straight and moist, and always looks well, his beard is of the same color, of which he wears the mustache and a tuft upon the chin; complexion ruddy, features neither large nor small, but well cut, with full jaw and chin, compressed mouth, straight nose, full, deep blue eyes, and a very mobile, emotional countenance. He always dresses remarkably well, and his manner is dignified, gentlemanly and commanding.'

Daniel Edgar Sickles

III Corps Commander. A New York politician with essentially no military experience before the war, Sickles was born in New York City on 20 October 1819. A Congressman from New York, he gained notoriety when he shot and killed his wife's lover not far from the White House. Defended by Edwin Stanton, later to become US Secretary of War, he was found not guilty by reason of insanity, the first time such a verdict had been produced by a US trial. He took his wife back after the incident, something that 'proper society' felt improper, and the couple were not received thereafter.

Although he was a Democrat and leader in Tammany Hall in New York, Sickles was loyal to the Union and raised a full brigade, the 'Excelsior Brigade', when the Civil War broke out. Lincoln was desperate to show bi-partisan support for the government and had him appointed a brigadier general of volunteers, ranking from 29 November 1862, in command of his brigade. Serving on the Peninsula and in the Antietam Campaign, he received divisional command for Fredericksburg and command of III Corps before Chancellorsville. There he advanced after seeing Confederates he felt to be retreating, a move that helped expose XI Corps to Jackson's famed attack.

Major General Daniel Sickles.

Despite his lack of military education, Sickles felt that he was, in terms of military abilities, at least as good if not better than his peers. He often disagreed with them and with his superiors, and could not be wholly trusted to follow orders if he felt he could do something better. At Gettysburg he did not like the position he had been assigned towards the middle of the Union line, preferring higher ground to his front. His advance put a large bulge in the line, and Longstreet's attack on 2 July on exactly that bulge threatened to break the Union line. Reinforced, III Corps, despite heavy losses, managed to return to their original position where they could halt the Confederate attacks. In that action Sickles was shot in the leg. His personal bravery was seen as he was observed leaving the field on a stretcher, boldly smoking a cigar as if at a dining-table. Later the leg was amputated, and he held no active command in that army again.

Staff officer Haskell echoed many in the army who felt that Sickles was 'neither born nor bred a soldier ... a man after show and notoriety, and newspaper fame, and the adulation of the mob!'

George Sykes

V Corps Commander. Born in Dover, the state capital of Delaware, on 9 October 1822, Sykes graduated in the US Military Academy Class of 1842. He served in the Seminole War as well as the Mexican War, where he earned brevet captain rank for gallantry. At the outbreak of the Civil War he was appointed major in the 14th US Infantry Regiment, commanding a battalion of Regular Army soldiers at the First Manassas. His command was one of the few to maintain discipline during the rout there. He was appointed brigadier general of volunteers on 28 September 1861, commanding a brigade and then a division of V Corps on the Peninsula. His command was largely made up of Regular Army regiments.

Sykes' men were in the midst of the Second Manassas, but played only a supporting role at Antietam and a minor role at Chancellorsville. When Meade was moved to command of the Army of the Potomac Sykes was given command of V Corps. Sykes' corps was one of the last on to the field at Gettysburg, but arrived on the Union left just in time to block Longstreet's destruction of III Corps and send troops to hold Little Round Top on the extreme Union right. But Meade grew disenchanted with Sykes, whom he felt to be slow in action after Gettysburg, and had him relieved of command.

Staff officer Haskell wrote that Sykes was 'a small, rather thin man, well dressed and gentlemanly, brown hair and beard, which he wears full, with a red, pinched, rough-looking skin, feeble blue eyes, long nose, with the general air of one who is weary and a little ill-natured'.

John Sedgwick

VI Corps Commander. One of the most popular officers in the high command of the Army of the Potomac, Sedgwick was born in the Connecticut Berkshires on 13 September 1813. After a period as a local schoolteacher, he entered the US Military Academy, graduating in the Class of 1837. He saw service against Native Americans in Florida, Georgia, and Oklahoma before serving in the Mexican War, where he earned brevets to captain and major. At the outbreak of the Civil War he was named colonel of the 2nd US Cavalry Regiment, replacing an officer who had resigned to join the Confederate Army.

Sedgwick was appointed brigadier general of volunteers on 31 August 1861, and served in the Peninsula Campaign. He was wounded there on 30 June 1862. On his return to the army he was made a major general of volunteers to rank from 4 July 1862. He was wounded three times leading his troops at Antietam. Returning to the army three months later he was given command first of IX Corps, then of VI Corps. At Chancellorsville his was an independent command that stormed Fredericksburg successfully but was unable to break through to the main army. His corps was the last on to the field at Gettysburg and was held essentially in reserve, suffering few casualties.

Staff officer Haskell wrote that Sedgwick was 'quite a heavy man, short, thickset and muscular, with florid complexion, dark, calm, straight-looking eyes, with full, heavyish features, which, with his eyes, have plenty of animation when he is aroused. He has a magnificent profile, well cut, with the nose and forehead forming almost a straight line, curly, short, chestnut hair and full beard, cut short, with a little gray in it. He dresses carelessly, but can look magnificently when he is well dressed. Like Meade, he looks and is honest and modest. You might see at once, why his men, because they love him, call him "Uncle John", not to his face, of course, but to themselves.'

Oliver Otis Howard

XI Corps Commander. Born in Leeds, Maine, on 8 November 1830, he was a graduate from Bowdoin College in 1850. Entering the US Military Academy immediately afterwards, he graduated four years later. Assigned to the Ordnance Department, he spent much of his pre-war career teaching mathematics at the Academy. At the outbreak of the Civil War he became colonel of the

3rd Maine Infantry, and commanded a brigade at the First Manassas. He was appointed brigadier general of volunteers from 3 September 1861, and commanded a brigade in the Peninsula Campaign. He was wounded at the Battle of Seven Pines and an arm was later amputated. Returning to the army, his command was held in reserve at the Second Manassas, but he took over Sedgwick's command at Antietam and led it at Fredericksburg. On 31 March 1863, he was named a major general and given command of XI Corps, which he led at Chancellorsville.

He and his immediate subordinates failed miserably at Chancellorsville. They refused to believe reports of an imminent Confederate attack, and failed to post adequate pickets to give the alarm. His command was routed there. He was noted riding around the field with a US flag tucked under his arm's stump trying unsuccessfully to rally his men. As his command was largely made up of German immigrant regiments, the fighting men were largely blamed for Howard's errors and he continued in command.

At Gettysburg again he displayed poor powers of decision, but again rallied men who had been driven out of the town on Cemetery Ridge. He afterwards felt that he had won the battle by halting the defeated men on these positions, which they managed to hold throughout the battle. Again, the German officers and men under his command received most of the blame for the early victory of the Confederate forces at Gettysburg, rather than Howard himself.

He was a devout and evangelical Christian. He was noted for being an extremely severe disciplinarian who would have a man punished to the maximum at first and then visit him in his tent to console and pray with him. Such actions did not endear him to his men.

Howard, according to staff officer Haskell, was 'medium in size, has nothing marked about him, is the youngest of them all, I think – has lost an arm in the war, has straight brown hair and beard, shaves his short upper lip, over which his nose slants down, dim blue eyes, and on the whole, appears a very pleasant, affable, well dressed little gentleman'.

Henry Warner Slocum XII Corps Commander. Born in up-state New York on 24 September 1827, he was a schoolteacher until he entered the US Military Academy from where he graduated in the Class of 1852. He served in the Seminole War, but later resigned to practise law in New York. He was a politician there while serving as a colonel in the New York State Militia before the war.

On 21 May 1861 Slocum was appointed colonel of the 27th New York Infantry, commanding it at the First Manassas where he was wounded. On his recovery he was made a brigadier general of volunteers and given brigade command. On 29 July 1862 he became major general of volunteers and was given divisional command. He led his troops on the Peninsula, in the Second Manassas, and Antietam. After Antietam he was given command of the newly formed XII Corps, which saw fierce fighting at Chancellorsville.

On the extreme right of the Union Army on 1 July, Slocum was actually senior major general on the field before Meade arrived, but declined to press for command there. Although his corps was the smallest on the field, his men protected a line from Culp's Hill across the Baltimore Pike.

Staff officer Haskell noted that Slocum was 'small, rather spare, with black, straight hair and beard, which latter is unshaven and thick, large, full, quick, black eyes, white skin, sharp nose, wide cheek bones, and hollow cheeks and small chin. His movements are quick and angular, and he dresses with a sufficient degree of elegance'.

Henry Jackson Hunt

Artillery Commander. He was born to a family of Regular Army officers in Detroit on 14 September 1819. A member of the US Military Academy Class of 1839, he achieved recognition, especially as an artillery officer, in Mexico, winning brevets of captain and major there. He was one of a board of three officers charged with the creation of a new system of light artillery tactics in 1860, and was named chief of artillery of the defences of Washington in the winter of 1861/62. He went from there to being chief of artillery in the Army of the Potomac for the Peninsula Campaign and was named brigadier general of volunteers after Antietam on 15 September 1862.

Hunt was greatly respected by those who served under him. A man of wide interests and knowledge, he was the top authority on artillery in the US Army at the time, and his tactics at Gettysburg were all the right ones, his only problems occurring when Hancock gave orders to batteries on his sector of the field.

Alfred Pleasonton

Cavalry Commander. A native of Washington, DC., born there on 7 July 1824, Pleasonton graduated in the US Military Academy Class of 1844, ranking seventh in his class of 25. He received a brevet for gallantry in the Mexican War and then saw service in the Seminole War and as commander of the 2nd US Dragoon Regiment. A major in the Peninsula Campaign, he was promoted to brigadier general of volunteers on 18 July 1862, and commanded a division of the Army of the Potomac's Cavalry Corps at Antietam, Fredericksburg, and Chancellorsville. He was named major general of volunteers on 22 June 1863, and given command of the Cavalry Corps, replacing George Stoneman whose raid behind enemy lines had done little for Hooker's main army at Chancellorsville.

Pleasonton was widely despised by subordinates and not a few peers as a highly political man who took credit for more than he actually deserved. He was seen more at higher headquarters than with his own troops, according to many. His performance at Gettysburg was undistinguished.

Staff officer Haskell described Pleasonton as 'quite a nice little dandy, with brown hair and beard, a straw hat with a little jockey rim, which he cocks upon one side of his head, with an unsteady eye, that looks slyly at you and then dodges'.

THE ARMY OF THE POTOMAC

The Army of the Potomac, the main Union force along the Atlantic seaboard, was essentially created by its first commander, Major General George B. McClellan, from the remnant of the army defeated at the First Manassas with additional volunteer regiments added as they arrived at its camps in the Washington area.

For the Gettysburg campaign the army comprised seven corps, each under a major general, and each having elements of artillery, cavalry, and infantry, plus a staff section and headquarters troops. The latter included the staff, provost marshal troops, three units of engineers, and signal corps detachments. There was also a Cavalry Corps, which had its own horse artillery, and an artillery reserve.

Each general officer was surrounded immediately by his personal staff, which was usually fairly small and all too often made up entirely of amateurs. There was no army staff training available, and each general was free to name his own staff members. Meade had his own son, George Gordon Meade III, assigned as a colonel aide-de-camp on his personal staff. When a general officer was removed from command, by wounds or politics, his staff were suddenly out of a job, unless retained by the incoming general, who often preferred his own staff, so any experience they'd gained was lost to the army. These men were largely responsible for passing on the general's orders to subordinate commanders. As a result most Civil War actions were marked by sloppy staff work. At Gettysburg, for example, poorly worded orders from headquarters resulted in a XII Corps division of 2,500 men leaving the field when they were most needed.

Beyond the general staff, there was the army's staff which included different department commanders.

Brigadier General Daniel Butterfield, a Hooker appointee to the position, was retained as the army's chief of staff. His job was to oversee the subordinate staff officers, passing his commander's orders to them as required, as well as passing on information from them to Meade. He was also responsible for drawing up movement orders, aided by several assistant adjutants general. He was wounded in the battle.

Brigadier General Rufus Ingalls, a West Pointer who had spent most of his military career as a quartermaster, was the army's chief quartermaster. He arrived on the field on 2 July and made immediate arrangements for supply routes via a branch road from Baltimore and at Frederick, Maryland, by the Baltimore and Ohio Railroad. According to his after-action report: 'Ample supplies of forage, clothing, and subsistence were received and issued to fill every necessary want without in any instance retarding military movements.'

Brigadier General Marsena Patrick was the army's provost marshal general. He commanded a Regular Army infantry battalion, a volunteer infantry regiment, and a collection of cavalry companies, both regular and volunteer. These men would largely be posted behind the front lines, both to prevent stragglers from leaving the line to reach the rear and to collect enemy prisoners of war. On 2 July he noted: 'I had my hands full, with the Prov. Guards to keep the Troops from breaking – It was hot work & I had several lines formed, so that very few succeeded in getting entirely through ...' The next day he 'organized a guard of Stragglers to keep nearly 2000 Prisoners all safe ...' Afterwards he reported processing 754 captured Confederate officers and 12,867 enlisted men.

Brigadier General Henry Benham, a West Pointer, commanded the army's engineer brigade, which was engaged chiefly in getting the army across the various rivers between its original base in Virginia into Pennsylvania.

Brigadier General Henry Hunt was the army's chief of artillery. In overall charge, Brigadier General Robert Tayler's artillery reserve reported directly to him for its orders. Hunt reported that 320 guns in all were available in the army during the battle, of which 108 were in the artillery reserve. 'The expenditure of ammunition in the three days amounted to 32,781 rounds, averaging over 100 rounds per gun.'

Lieutenant John Edie was acting chief ordnance officer during the battle. Besides keeping the fighting men's weapons in good repair, his main job was collecting captured enemy munitions, which were forwarded by corps ordnance officers to his headquarters.

Dr. Jonathan Letterman was the army's medical director, and he oversaw the deployment of more than 650 medical officers, mostly assigned at regimental level, who were gathered together in central hospitals in battles such as Gettysburg, and an Ambulance Corps. The latter was the creation of Dr. Letterman, and consisted of trained personnel, marked with green cap bands, who picked up wounded men in the field and brought them back to field aid stations in specially equipped ambulances. The army's Medical Department was aided in its hospitals by civilians in the quasi-official US Sanitary Commission and US Christian Commission.

Colonel George Henry Sharpe was head of the army's Bureau of Military Information. This had been set up by Meade's predecessor, Hooker, and was in charge of gathering intelligence, from spies and questioning prisoners, and reporting findings to the commanding general. It was only 18-men strong when Meade took over the army, but had been successful in learning much about the Army of Northern Virginia. His group made a major intelligence breakthrough which helped Meade plan for 3 July; Sharpe reported on the afternoon of the 2nd that they had learned from interrogating prisoners that at this point Lee had essentially used every unit in his army except Pickett's Division. Meade, knowing that he still had V, VI and XII Corps largely unblooded, could more confidently decide to stay and fight as a result.

Captain Lemuel Norton was the army's chief signal officer. He was in charge of teams of Signal Corps officers and enlisted men assigned to different corps headquarters who signalled back and forth between one another and with army headquarters by torches, flags, and telegraphs. These men often found themselves in the advance of the army, as for example when on 2 July as Longstreet's men moved to the attack, the only Union forces on Little Round Top were a signals team. As a result, their duty was dangerous and during the battle three officers and six flagmen were captured by Confederates.

Each corps was commanded by a major general who had a staff that was similar in composition to the army staff. Most corps contained three divisions, each with a similar staff, and supposedly commanded by a major general although often brigadier generals filled in. Each division had several brigades, each with a similar staff and supposedly commanded by a brigadier general, although many were commanded by colonels. The Army of the Potomac at Gettysburg had 51 infantry brigades in the field, each numbering about 1,000 to 2,000 officers and men. Each brigade was made up of a number of regiments or battalions (a regiment had ten companies and was commanded by a colonel, while a battalion had fewer companies and was commanded by a lieutenant colonel or major). The word 'battalion' was often used for regiment in period writings. The average infantry regiment in the army in April 1863 numbered 433 present for duty, out of the authorised strength of 900 to 1,000.

Each corps was also assigned a number of artillery batteries, usually five (VI Corps had eight; XII Corps had four), with one Regular Army battery assigned to each corps artillery battalion. A corps chief of artillery commanded each battalion. Each battery had six guns and was divided into three sections of two guns each. Each section was led by a lieutenant, while a captain served as battery commander. The corps chief of artillery also commanded an artillery ammunition train which carried 270 rounds per gun. A field report of 30 June shows that the Army of the Potomac had 69 batteries, with 362 guns (Hunt later reported 320 guns although, in fact, the army seems to have had about 411 guns available), 217 officers, and 7,329 enlisted men.

Hooker organised the army's Cavalry Corps in February 1863. According to a field report of 25 June, it consisted of 703 officers and 12,411 enlisted men.

A consolidated field report for the Army of the Potomac of 30 June indicates 6,629 officers and 97,627 enlisted men of all branches present for duty, giving an aggregate of 117,930 all ranks. However, the same field report indicates that the army had on the line, equipped, and ready for action only 5,286 officers and 71,922 enlisted men. Even these figures do not accurately reflect the combat, front line strength of the army since they include many men who were actually assigned as teamsters, ambulance drivers, clerks, cooks, etc. One regiment, for example, had a 'pres-

ent' strength of 525 men, but actually had only 172 officers and men ready in line to fight. In fact, the effective strength of the Army of the Potomac at Gettysburg appears to have been about 85,500.

While in Pennsylvania they would all be fighting harder to defend their home territory, the army started the campaign in relatively poor spirits. Private Wilbur Fisk, 2nd Vermont Infantry, wrote to his home newspaper on 10 June 1863: 'The boys were not in good spirits ... Perhaps, for the sake of telling a good story, I ought to say we were in the best of spirits – anxious to meet the foe – confident of success, and with unbounded faith in General Hooker – but I shall say no such thing ... Perhaps this grim determination on the part of the men, would be considered the "best of spirits" by those who are judges of human nature.'

This point on East Cemetery Hill was part of the gun line of Battery B, 1st Pennsylvania Light Artillery. Confederates of Hays' and Avery's brigades charged towards this position from the left at about 8 p.m. on 1 July. The gun is a 3in Ordnance rifle.

HEADQUARTERS

Signal Corps

Provost Marshal's Command: 2nd, 6th Pennsylvania Cavalry Regiments; detachments from the 1st, 2nd, 5th, 6th US Cavalry Regiments

Engineer Brigade: 15th, 50th New York Volunteer Engineer Regiments; US. Engineer Battalion

I CORPS

Headquarters: Co. L, 1st Maine Cavalry Regiment

First Division

First (Iron) Brigade: 19th Indiana, 24th Michigan, 2nd, 6th, 7th Wisconsin Infantry Regiments

Second Brigade: 7th Indiana, 56th Pennsylvania (nine companies), 76th, 84th (14th Militia), 95th, 147th New York Infantry Regiments

Second Division

First Brigade: 16th Maine, 13th Massachusetts, 107th Pennsylvania, 94th, 104th New York Infantry Regiments

Second Brigade: 12th Massachusetts, 83rd (9th Militia), 97th New York, 11th, 88th, 90th Pennsylvania Infantry Regiments

Third Division

First Brigade: 80th (20th Militia) New York, 121st, 142nd, 151st Pennsylvania Infantry Regiments

Second Brigade: 143rd, 149th, 150th Pennsylvania Infantry Regiments

Third Brigade: 13th, 14th, 16th Vermont Infantry Regiments

Corps Artillery Brigade: 2nd (B) Battery, Maine Light Artillery; 5th (E) Battery, Maine Light Artillery; Batteries L, E, 1st New York Light Artillery; Battery B, 1st Pennsylvania Light Artillery; Battery B, 4th US Artillery Regiment

II CORPS

Headquarters: Companies D, K, 6th New York Cavalry Regiment

First Division

First Brigade: 5th New Hampshire, 61st New York, 81st, 148th Pennsylvania Infantry Regiments

Second (Irish) Brigade: 28th Massachusetts, 116th Pennsylvania (four companies); 63rd (two companies), 69th (two companies), 88th (two companies) New York Infantry Regiments

Third Brigade: 140th Pennsylvania, 52nd, 57th, 66th New York Infantry Regiments

Fourth Brigade: 2nd Delaware, 64th New York, 27th Connecticut (two companies), 53rd, 145th Pennsylvania (seven companies) Infantry Regiments

Second Division

First Brigade: 19th Maine, 15th Massachusetts, 1st Minnesota, 82nd (2nd Militia) New York Infantry Regiments, 2nd Company Minnesota Sharpshooters

Second (Philadelphia) Brigade: 69th, 71st, 72nd, 106th Pennsylvania Infantry Regiments

Third Brigade: 19th, 20th Massachusetts, 7th Michigan, 42nd, 59th New York (four companies) Infantry Regiments

Unattached: 1st Company, Massachusetts Sharpshooters

Third Division

First Brigade: 14th Indiana, 4th, 8th Ohio, 7th West Virginia Infantry Regiments

Second Brigade: 14th Connecticut, 1st Delaware, 12th New Jersey, 108th New York Infantry Regiments, 10th New York Infantry Battalion

Third Brigade: 39th (four companies), 111th, 125th, 126th New York Infantry Regiments

Divisional Artillery Brigade: Battery B, 1st New York Light and 14th New York Battery; Batteries A, B, 1st Rhode Island Light Artillery; Battery L, 1st US Artillery Regiment; Battery A, 4th US Artillery Regiment

III CORPS

First Division

First Brigade: 37th (eight companies), 63rd, 68th, 105th, 114th (Collis' Zouaves), 141st Pennsylvania Infantry Regiments

Second Brigade: 20th Indiana, 3rd, 4th Maine, 86th, 124th New York, 99th Pennsylvania Infantry Regiments, 1st, 2nd (eight companies) US Sharpshooter Regiments

Third Brigade: 17th Maine, 3rd, 5th Michigan, 40th New York, 110th Pennsylvania (six companies) Infantry Regiments

Second Division

First Brigade: 1st, 11th, 16th Massachusetts, 12th New Hampshire, 11th New Jersey, 26th Pennsylvania Infantry Regiments

Second Brigade: 70th, 71st, 72nd, 73rd, 74th, 120th New York Infantry Regiments

Third Brigade: 2nd New Hampshire, 5th, 6th, 7th, 8th New Jersey, 115th Pennsylvania Infantry Regiments

Divisional Artillery Brigade: 2nd Battery, New Jersey Light Artillery; Battery D, 1st New York Light Artillery; 4th Battery, New York Light Artillery; Battery E, 1st Rhode Island Light Artillery; Battery K, 4th US Artillery Regiment

V CORPS

Headquarters: Companies D, E, 12th New York Infantry; Companies D, H, 17th Pennsylvania Cavalry Regiments

First Division

First Brigade: 18th, 22nd Massachusetts, 1st Michigan, 118th Pennsylvania Infantry Regiments

Second Brigade: 9th, 32nd Massachusetts, 4th Michigan, 62nd Pennsylvania Infantry Regiments

Third Brigade: 20th Maine, 16th Michigan, 44th New York, 83rd Pennsylvania Infantry Regiments

Second Division

First Brigade: 3rd (six companies), 4th (four companies), 6th (five companies), 12th (eight companies), 14th (eight companies) US Infantry Regiments

Second Brigade: 2nd (six companies), 7th (four companies), 10th (three companies), 11th (six companies), 17th (seven companies) US Infantry Regiments

Third Brigade: 140th, 146th New

York, 91st, 155th Pennsylvania Infantry Regiments

Third Division

First Brigade: 1st (nine companies), 2nd, 6th, 13th Regiments of Pennsylvania Reserves

Third Brigade: 5th, 9th, 10th, 11th, 12th (nine companies) Regiments of Pennsylvania Reserves

Divisional Artillery Brigade: Battery C (3rd Battery), Massachusetts Light Artillery; Battery C, 1st New York Light Artillery; Battery L, 1st Ohio Light Artillery; Batteries D, I, 5th US Artillery Regiment

VI CORPS

Headquarters: Co. L, 1st New Jersey Cavalry; Co. H, 1st Pennsylvania Cavalry Regiments

First Division

Provost Guard: 4th New Jersey Infantry Regiment (three companies)

First Brigade: 1st, 2nd, 3rd, 15th New Jersey Infantry Regiments

Second Brigade: 5th Maine, 121st New York, 95th, 96th Pennsylvania Infantry Regiments

Third Brigade: 6th Maine, 49th (four companies), 119th Pennsylvania, 5th Wisconsin Infantry Regiments

Second Division

Second Brigade: 2nd, 3rd, 4th, 5th, 6th Vermont Infantry Regiments

Third Brigade: 7th Maine (six companies), 33rd (detachment), 43rd, 49th, 77th New York, 61st Pennsylvania Infantry Regiments

Third Division

First Brigade: 65th, 67th, 122nd New York, 23rd, 82nd Pennsylvania Infantry Regiments

Second Brigade: 7th, 10th, 37th Massachusetts, 2nd Rhode Island Infantry Regiments

Third Brigade: 62nd New York, 93rd, 98th, 139th Pennsylvania Infantry Regiments

Divisional Artillery Brigade: Battery A (1st Battery), Massachusetts Light Artillery; 1st, 3rd Batteries, New York Light Artillery; Batteries C, G, 1st Rhode Island Light Artillery; Batteries D, G, 2nd US Artillery Regiment; Battery F, 5th US Artillery Regiment

XI CORPS

Headquarters: Companies I, K, 1st Indiana Cavalry; one company, 8th New York Infantry Regiments

First Division

First Brigade: 41st (nine companies), 54th, 68th New York, 153rd Pennsylvania Infantry Regiments

Second Brigade: 17th Connecticut, 25th, 75th, 107th Ohio Infantry Regiments

Second Division

First Brigade: 134th, 154th New York, 27th, 73rd Pennsylvania Infantry Regiments

Second Brigade: 33rd Massachusetts, 136th New York, 55th, 73rd Ohio Infantry Regiments

Third Division

First Brigade: 82nd Illinois, 45th, 157th New York, 61st Ohio, 74th

Pennsylvania Infantry Regiments
Second Brigade: 58th, 119th New York, 82nd Ohio, 75th Pennsylvania, 26th Wisconsin Infantry Regiments
Artillery Brigade: Battery I, 1st New York Light Artillery; 13th Battery, New York Light Artillery; Batteries I, K, 1st Ohio Light Artillery; Battery G, 4th US Artillery Regiment

XII CORPS
Provost Guard: 10th Maine Infantry Regiment (four companies)

First Division
First Brigade: 5th, 20th Connecticut, 3rd Maryland, 123rd, 145th New York, 46th Pennsylvania Infantry Regiments
Second Brigade: 1st Maryland (Potomac Home Brigade), 1st Maryland (Eastern Shore), 150th New York Infantry Regiments
Third Brigade: 27th Indiana, 2nd Massachusetts, 13th New Jersey, 107th New York, 3rd Wisconsin Infantry Regiments

Second Division
First Brigade: 5th, 7th, 29th, 66th Ohio, 28th, 147th (eight companies) Pennsylvania Infantry Regiments
Second Brigade: 29th, 109th, 111th Pennsylvania Infantry Regiments
Third Brigade: 60th, 78th, 102nd, 137th, 149th New York Infantry Regiments
Artillery Brigade: Battery M, 1st New York Light Artillery; Battery E, Pennsylvania Light Artillery; Battery F, 4th US Artillery Regiment; Battery K, 5th US Artillery Regiment

CAVALRY CORPS

First Division
First Brigade: 8th, 12th (four companies) Illinois, 3rd Indiana, 8th New York Cavalry Regiments
Second Brigade: 6th, 9th New York, 17th Pennsylvania, 3rd West Virginia (two companies) Cavalry Regiments
Reserve Brigade: 6th Pennsylvania (Rush's Lancers), 1st, 2nd, 5th, 6th US Cavalry Regiments

Second Division
Headquarters: Co. A, 1st Ohio Cavalry Regiment
First Brigade: 1st Maryland (eight companies), 1st Massachusetts, 1st New Jersey, 1st, 3rd Pennsylvania Cavalry Regiments; Co. A, Purnell (Maryland) Legion; Battery H, 3rd Pennsylvania Artillery (one section)
Third Brigade: 1st Maine (ten companies), 10th New York, 4th, 16th Pennsylvania Cavalry Regiments

Third Division
Headquarters: Co. C, 1st Ohio Cavalry Regiment
First Brigade: 5th New York, 18th Pennsylvania, 1st Vermont, 1st West Virginia (ten companies) Cavalry Regiments
Second (Wolverine) Brigade: 1st, 5th, 6th, 7th (ten companies) Michigan Cavalry Regiments

Horse Artillery
First Brigade: 9th Michigan Battery; 6th New York Battery; Batteries B, L, M, 2nd US Artillery Regiment; Battery E, 4th US Artillery Regiment
Second Brigade: Batteries E, G, K, 1st

US Artillery Regiment; Battery A, 2nd US Artillery Regiment

Army Artillery Reserve
Headquarters: Co. C, 32nd Massachusetts Infantry Regiment
Train Guard: 4th New Jersey Infantry Regiment (seven companies)

First Regular Brigade: Battery H, 1st US; Batteries F, K, 3rd US; Battery C, 4th US; Battery C, 5th US Artillery Regiments
First Volunteer Brigade: Battery E (5th Battery), Massachusetts Light Artillery; 9th Battery, Massachusetts Light Artillery; 10th New York Battery; 15th Battery, New York Light Artillery; Batteries C, F, Pennsylvania Light Artillery
Second Volunteer Brigade: 2nd Battery, Connecticut Light Artillery; 5th Battery, New York Light Artillery
Third Volunteer Brigade: 1st Battery, New Hampshire Light Artillery; Battery H, 1st Ohio Light Artillery; Batteries F, G, 1st Pennsylvania Light Artillery; Battery C, West Virginia Light Artillery
Fourth Volunteer Brigade: Battery F (6th Battery), Maine Light Artillery; Battery A, Maryland Light Artillery; 1st Battery, New Jersey Light Artillery; Batteries G, K, 1st New York Light Artillery; 11th New York Battery

LEADERS OF THE ARMY OF NORTHERN VIRGINIA

Robert Edward Lee Army of Northern Virginia Commander. Son of the legendary Revolutionary War general 'Light Horse Harry' Lee, he was born in Stratford, Virginia, on 19 January 1807. With an unblemished record at the US Military Academy, where he graduated second in the Class of 1829, he was assigned to the Corps of Engineers and spent much time on fortification building until the Mexican War when he was assigned to the staff of commanding general Winfield Scott. He was brevetted colonel in that war, then returned to serve as Superintendent of the US Military Academy and lieutenant colonel of the 2nd US Cavalry Regiment.

On the Civil War's outbreak he resigned his commission to accept appointment as commander of Virginia's forces, then transferred, when that state joined the Confederacy, into the Confederate Army as a brigadier general and then full general, ranking from 14 June 1861. His first field command was in West Virginia where, failing to handle feuding subordinates and having an ill-equipped force, he fared badly. He was then sent to oversee fortifications along the southern coast, returning to Richmond to advise the president. After the wounding of Joseph Johnston and nervous breakdown of G. W. Smith, he assumed command of the force around Richmond that he named the Army of Northern Virginia. After seeing to its reorganisation, he showed his aggressive nature by attacking a retreating McClellan in several days of operations that cost his army large losses. The effectiveness of his troops in the attack was always marred by sloppy staff work, and he never succeeded in eradicating this flaw.

After seeing McClellan tied down outside Richmond, he turned to crush another attempt to move towards Richmond from the north in the Second Manassas, then invaded Maryland in an attempt to buy time for Virginia's farmers and to gather recruits and supplies in Maryland. Finding his plans discovered and Federal forces closing in, he chose to fight at Antietam, his back to the Potomac. By brilliantly moving forces around to meet piecemeal threats, and thanks in part to the lucky arrival of A. P. Hill from Harpers Ferry, he managed to fight the battle to a stand-off.

After returning to Virginia, he fought an easy battle at Fredericksburg, then, his army badly outnumbered, fought a brilliant battle at Chancellorsville where he daringly divided his smaller force to turn the Federal flank. However, his health at this time was not at all good. Apparently he had suffered a mild heart attack in early 1863 and from then on was weaker and more desperate.

General Robert E. Lee. (*Military Images* Magazine)

Lee was fiercely aggressive, believing that the Confederacy had to make Northern families suffer in order to persuade them abandon their attempt to keep the Southern states in the Union. At Gettysburg Longstreet suggested moving around the Union left to a position where Meade would be forced to attack on Southern terms. 'No,' Longstreet recalled Lee saying, 'there they are there in position, and I am going to whip them or they are going to whip me.' Such an aggressive spirit almost always cost the Army of Northern Virginia more casualties than it inflicted, yet his men deeply loved Lee almost to a man.

Having created his plan of action and issued his orders, Lee spent little time in battlefield control. A visiting British officer, Arthur Fremantle, was near Lee and A. P. Hill during the attack of 3 July and saw him: '... looking through his fieldglass – sometimes talking to Hill and sometimes to Colonel Long of his staff. But generally he sat quite alone on the stump of a tree. What I remarked especially was, that during the whole time the firing continued, he only sent one message, and only received one report. It is evidently his system to arrange the plan thoroughly with the three corps commanders, and then leave them the duty of modifying and carrying it out to the best of their abilities.' This worked well with someone capable of independent action such as Stonewall Jackson, but Jackson was not at Gettysburg and the three corps commanders were not up to this type of management style.

Fremantle described Lee as 'almost without exception, the handsomest man of his age I ever saw. He is fifty-six years old, tall, broad shouldered, very well made, well set up – thorough soldier in appearance; and his manners are most courteous and full of dignity. He is a perfect gentleman in every respect. I imagine no man has so few enemies, or is so universally esteemed ... He has none of the small vices, such as smoking, drinking, chewing, or swearing, and his bitterest enemy never accused him of any greater ones.'

James Longstreet I Corps Commander. Born in the Edgefield District of South Carolina on 8 January 1821, Longstreet graduated from the US Military Academy's Class of 1842. Having earned two brevets for gallantry in the Mexican War, he also served in various campaigns against Native Americans, but then went on staff duty as a paymaster. When he resigned from the US Army on 1 June 1861 he was serving as a paymaster with the rank of major. He was appointed a Confederate brigadier general on 17 June 1861, and commanded a brigade at Blackburn's Ford and First Manassas. On 7 October 1861 he was promoted to major general, commanding a division and, when Lee divided the Army of Northern Virginia into corps, the first of those. He fought well at the Second Manassas and Antietam, although there he wasted valuable command time when he and his staff manned a cannon whose crew had all been wounded or killed.

Lieutenant General James Longstreet, a woodcut from *Harper's Weekly*.

Early in the war he was fond of a drink or two and a sharp game of cards. In late 1861, however, he lost his wife and three of his children to scarlet fever within a week. Thereafter he was not as cheerful as he had been. He became rather a devoted communicant of the Episcopal Church. Somewhat hard of hearing, he had always been silent, especially in large groups, and strangers found him even colder and more distant than before.

Longstreet always sought an independent command, and in 1862–63 he managed to get his corps sent south of the James River, though he didn't do much good in reaching his objectives nor was he available for Chancellorsville. Moreover, he tended to be slow, especially in making moves of which he did not fully approve. Still, Lee greatly trusted in him, calling him 'my old warhorse'.

Brigadier General G. Moxley Sorrel served on Longstreet's staff and later described him as being 'very handsome, tall and well proportioned, strong and active, a superb horseman and with an unsurpassed soldierly bearing, his features and expression fairly matched; eyes, glint steel blue, deep and piercing; a full brown beard, head well shaped and poised. The worst feature was the mouth, rather coarse; it was partly hidden, however, by his ample beard.'

George Edward Pickett

I Corps Divisional Commander. George Pickett, whose name would become forever linked with Gettysburg, was born in Richmond, Virginia, on 28 January 1825. He graduated last in the Class of 1846 from the US Military Academy. He saw brave service in the Mexican War, where he became friends with fellow subaltern James 'Old Pete' Longstreet, earning two brevets for gallantry. He then served in the west, notably in 1859 on San Juan Island, Washington Territory, which was in dispute with Great Britain at that time. The British who faced him there, however, found his conduct admirable and the affair ended peacefully.

Resigning from the US Army, he was commissioned a Confederate colonel and assigned to the defences of the Lower Rappahannock. He was promoted to brigadier general ranking from 14 January 1862, and led an all-Virginia brigade on the Peninsula where he was badly wounded at Gaines Mill. Rejoining his command after recovery, he served at Antietam and was made a major general on 10 October 1862. He was then given command of an all-Virginia division in Longstreet's Corps, the smallest division in the Army of Northern Virginia.

Staff officer Sorrel described Pickett as, 'A very singular figure indeed! A medium-size, well-built man, straight, erect, and in well-fitting uniform, an elegant riding-whip in hand, his appearance was distinguished and striking. But the head, the hair were extraordinary. Long ringlets flowed

Major General George Pickett. (*Military Images* Magazine)

loosely over his shoulders, trimmed and highly perfumed; his beard likewise was curling and giving out the scents of Araby.'

Richard Stoddard Ewell II Corps Commander. Born in Georgetown, District of Columbia, on 8 February 1817, Ewell was a member the US Military Academy Class of 1840. He earned a brevet for gallantry in the Mexican War and served in the south-west until he resigned from the US Army on 7 May 1861. Commissioned a brigadier general in the Provisional Army of the Confederate States on 17 June 1861, he became a major general on 4 January 1862, leading a division in Stonewall Jackson's Valley Campaign. He was badly wounded at the Battle of Groveton and a leg had to be amputated. Afterwards he wore a wooden replacement, but his health, never all that good to begin with, became even worse. On the death of Jackson he was given command of II Corps and promoted to lieutenant general on 23 May 1863.

Lieutenant General Richard S. Ewell. (*Military Images* Magazine)

He was somewhat of a disappointment as a corps commander; having been bold and aggressive as a brigade and divisional commander, he now seems to have become more cautious. Certainly his failure to capture Cemetery Ridge on the evening of 1 July was, at best, controversial.

Staff officer Sorrel described Ewell: 'Bald as an eagle, he looked like one; had a piercing eye and lisping speech ... To uncommon courage and activity he added a fine military instinct, which could make him a good second in command in any army.' Fremantle described Ewell as having 'a bald head, a prominent nose, and rather a haggard, sickly face. Having so lately lost his leg above the knee, he is still a complete cripple, and falls off his horse occasionally. Directly he dismounts he has to be put on crutches.'

Ambrose Powell Hill III Corps Commander. A. P. Hill was born in Culpeper, Virginia, on 9 November 1825. A member of the US Military Academy's Class of 1847, he saw service in Florida and Mexico. He resigned from the US Army on 1 March 1861, to take a position as colonel commanding the 13th Virginia Infantry

Regiment. He was promoted to brigadier general on 26 February 1862, and led a brigade and then a division well in the Peninsula Campaign. He was promoted to major general on 26 May 1862. After Stonewall Jackson was wounded at Chancellorsville, he turned his command over to Hill. Shortly afterwards Hill was apparently struck by a shell fragment and, unable to walk, passed the command to J. E. B. Stuart. On 24 May 1863, Hill was promoted to lieutenant general and given command of the Army of Northern Virginia's new III Corps.

Lieutenant General A. P. Hill. (*Military Images* Magazine)

Hill was an aggressive soldier in battle, often a bit too much so. This was valuable, as when he brought up his troops on a forced march from Harpers Ferry to Sharpsburg just in time to save Lee's army, and when he arrived at Cedar Mountain to turn the tide against the Federal attack. But he sometimes failed to make necessary reconnaissance before committing his troops to battle. He struck early in the Seven Days fighting, when Jackson failed to make his attack, and sustained heavy casualties. He would go on to do that again after Gettysburg.

Moreover, Hill, who apparently had contracted a venereal disease just after leaving West Point, was often ill and not available when needed. Although he was in command of the centre at Gettysburg, he seems in fact to have been largely a non-participant in that battle. While one of his divisional commanders was opening the battle, Hill was miles away in an ambulance at Cashtown. On 3 July Lee gave the main assault command to Longstreet, although most troops in that attack would come from Hill's Corps.

Staff officer Sorrel, who found himself in the midst of a controversy between Hill and Longstreet after the Peninsula Campaign, described Hill as a '... man of medium height, a light, good figure, and most pleasing soldierly appearance. He surely handled his division on all occasions with great ability and courage and justly earned high reputation. When Lee created the Third Army Corps he placed him in command of it, and it was thought Hill did not realise in that high position all that was hoped of him.'

William Nelson Pendleton Artillery Commander. Born in Richmond, Virginia, on 26 December 1809, he graduated from the US Military Academy Class of 1830, but resigned three years later to enter a seminary. Ordained an Episcopal minister, he was called to Grace Church, Lexington, Virginia, where he was rector at the outbreak of the Civil War. He accepted command of the local Rockbridge Artillery as a captain, but was soon appointed colonel and chief of artillery in Joseph E. Johnston's Army of the Potomac. He remained in this post when Lee assumed command and was promoted to brigadier general on 26 March 1862.

Pendleton, an older man in an army of youngsters, largely confined his contributions to administration rather than tactical command. It is significant that Lee did not give him command of the artillery in preparation for Pickett's Charge but chose Longstreet's younger corps artillery commander, E. P. Alexander. Indeed, although Pendleton offered the use of some of Hill's Corps' guns to Alexander, he did little to oversee the artillery attack. Alexander later wrote that there 'a great opportunity was lost of using the artillery of Ewell's corps to enfilade many of the batteries which fired upon Pickett's charge, & that the fault of this lay primarily with Gen. Pendleton, Gen. Lee's chief of artillery. He was too old & had been too long out of army life to be thoroughly up to all the opportunities of his position.'

The British visitor Fremantle noted that Pendleton 'unites the military and clerical professions together, and continues to preach whenever he gets a chance. On these occasions he wears a surplice over his uniform.'

Jame Ewell Brown Stuart Cavalry Corps Commander. 'JEB' Stuart was born in Patrick County, Virginia, on 6 February 1833. A graduate from the US Military Academy in 1854, he saw service on the frontier where he was badly wounded. He resigned from the US Army to accept command of the 1st Virginia Cavalry as its colonel when Virginia seceded from the Union. Leading this unit brilliantly at First Manassas, he was promoted brigadier general on 24 September 1861. Appointed commander of the army's cavalry, he led a detachment around the Federal army on the Peninsula, winning much popular fame. He was promoted to major general on 25 July 1862, and given command of the army's Cavalry Division, which was later made into the Cavalry Corps, but he never achieved the rank of lieutenant general, much though he sought it.

He was a mass of contradictions. A teetotaller and devout Episcopalian who attended one of that Church's general conventions, he loved parties, song, and young women. He sought fame and adoration more than perhaps any other high Confederate commander. He was noted as being able to provide excellent intelligence of enemy movements and fought well. But in the Gettysburg Campaign, smarting from a close-fought Brandy Station battle, he failed to keep Lee informed of Union movements, instead chasing fame by capturing a large Union wagon train which he insisted on keeping with him although it slowed his column down badly. He received, and deserved, much of the blame for Lee's loss at Gettysburg, one of the few occasions when he felt the weight of Lee's anger.

Major General J. E. B. Stuart. (National Archives)

One of his staff officers, John Esten Cooke, later wrote: 'His frame was low and athletic – close knit and of very great strength and endurance ... His countenance was striking ... the forehead broad, lofty ... the nose prominent, and inclining to "Roman", with large and mobile nostrils; the lips covered with a heavy brown moustache, curled upward at the ends; the chin by a large beard of the same colour, which descended upon the wearer's breast ... eyes ... clear, penetrating, and of a brilliant blue ... He wore a brown felt hat looped up with a star, and ornamented with an ebon feather; a double-breasted jacket always open and buttoned back; gray waistcoat and pantaloons; and boots to the knee, decorated with small spurs, which he wore even in dancing ... on marches he threw over his shoulder his gray cavalry cape ... [and] a beautiful yellow sash, whose folds he would carefully wrap around his waist, skillfully tying the ends on the left side so that the tassels fell full in view ...'

THE ARMY OF NORTHERN VIRGINIA

As most top officials in the Confederate government and military had come from the same sort of background in the US government and military, it comes as no surprise that the Confederate Army was basically a copy of the US Army. There were only slight differences, as, for example, the US Army had an Ordnance Department and a Corps of Artillery; the Confederate artillery handled both jobs. Likewise the US Inspector General's and Adjutant General's departments were merged into one by the Confederates. Otherwise, the basic combat units were essentially the same in organisation and equipment.

The Army of Northern Virginia's staff was described by Moxley Sorrel as 'small and efficient', but in many ways it was too small to oversee the running of such a large force. Sorrel later wrote that: 'Four majors (afterwards lieutenant-colonels and colonels) did his principal work. Walter Taylor, from the Virginia Military Institute, was adjutant general, and better could not be found for this important post.

'Charles Venable, a scholar and mathematician, and with some study of strategy, together with Charles Marshall, a distinguished lawyer ... did much of the correspondence under dictation ... [Colonel Armistead L.] Long, of the old Army, a close friend of the General, was ranked as military secretary and did various duties. [By Gettysburg] Brig.-Gen R. H. Chilton, A[cting] A[djutant] G[eneral], was assigned to confidential duties with the General, and was sometimes called chief of staff [he was named the army's inspector general in October 1862]. But Lee really had no such chief about him. The officer practically nearest its duties was his extremely efficient adjutant general, W. H. Taylor. Such, with the addition of several lieutenants serving as aides-de-camp, made up Lee's personal staff.'

Lieutenant Colonel James L. Corley served as the army's chief quartermaster, busy largely during the Pennsylvania campaign in impressing much needed supplies from local residents. Confederate quartermasters also served as paymasters, unlike the US Army paymasters who were in an independent department. Lieutenant Colonel Robert G. Cole was the army's chief commissary officer, and he, also, was greatly involved in impressing Pennsylvania's bounty for army use. Major Henry Young was the army's judge advocate general. Major D. B. Bridgeford, commander of the 1st Virginia Battalion, was the army's provost marshal. Captain J. T. Bernard was in charge of the ordnance train.

Lieutenant Colonel Jeremy Gilmer had been the chief engineer for the army in 1862, but he ended up heading the Engineer Department in Richmond, leaving the army without a chief staff engineer for the Gettysburg campaign. It would not be until the autumn of 1863 that Lieutenant Colonel William Smith would assume that position. In the meantime, maps of the Pennsylvania area were prepared by a civilian volunteer, Jed Hotchkiss, who had earlier served Stonewall Jackson.

Surgeon Lafayette Guild was the army's medical director and he felt that: 'As a body of professional gentlemen [the army's surgeons] compare favorably with any other similar organization upon this continent ...' The Medical Department also oversaw the ambulance corps, made up of two men from each regiment who were marked with red cap insignia for easy battlefield identification. After Gettysburg a civilian organisation, the Richmond Ambulance Committee, helped the army's medical department by moving wounded from Winchester, Virginia, to hospitals in the Richmond area.

William Pendleton was chief of artillery, with the general supervision of fifteen battalions, comprising more than 69 batteries, each generally with a complement of four guns, as opposed to the six in the Army of the Potomac. Lee's army had about 280 guns available, including 23 captured in the Valley on the way north and another 28 at Harpers Ferry: In all 164 guns would see action in the battle. J. E. B. Stuart was Cavalry Corps commander, with eight brigades plus Imboden's semi-independent mounted command and a 6-battery battalion of horse artillery with 24 guns. The army did not have an official chief signals officer, although the Confederates did have a small Signal Corps set up much as the Federal one. The Confederate Signal Corps, headquartered in Richmond, also supplied Lee with intelligence about his enemy.

Except for the Cavalry Corps, each corps was commanded by a lieutenant general, and consisted of divisions commanded by major generals, brigades commanded by brigadier generals (colonels sometimes having to assume command), and artillery battalions commanded by majors. There were 37 infantry brigades in the Army of Northern Virginia, fewer than in the Army of the Potomac. Returns dated 31 May 1863, show that the Army of Northern Virginia consisted of 6,116 officers and 68,343 enlisted men, for an aggregate present of 88,735. In fact, the total effectives of the Army of Northern Virginia at Gettysburg appear to have been about 75,000.

While, however, the Army of the Potomac had the advantage in numbers and guns, the Army of Northern Virginia was its superior in terms of morale. It had just won dramatic victories at Fredericksburg and Chancellorsville, where it was even more outnumbered. Tally Simpson, a private in the 3rd South Carolina Infantry, wrote to his sister on 26 June 1863, 'Yes, we are again in Maryland, and I trust that ere we return, the grand object for which we came shall be accomplished, and we may all soon return to our homes in peace. Ewell is already in Pennsylvania and we are fast following ... The signs of times are cheering, and I am hoping for grand results from all quarters. Our army is strong and in fine spirits, and has the most implicit confidence in Genl. Lee.'

HEADQUARTERS

Co. C, 39th Virginia Cavalry Battalion

FIRST (LONGSTREET'S) CORPS

McLaws' Division

Kershaw's Brigade: 2nd, 3rd, 7th, 8th, 15th South Carolina Infantry Regiments, 3rd South Carolina Infantry Battalion

Barksdale's Brigade: 13th, 17th, 18th, 21st Mississippi Infantry Regiments

Semmes' Brigade: 10th, 50th, 51st, 53rd Georgia Infantry Regiments

Wofford's Brigade: 16th, 18th, 24th Georgia Infantry Regiments, Infantry of Cobb's (Georgia) and Phillips' (Georgia) Legions

Divisional Artillery: Co. A, 10th North Carolina Regiment (Battery A, 1st North Carolina Artillery Regiment); Pulaski (Georgia) Artillery; 1st Co., Richmond Howitzers; Troup (Georgia) Artillery

Pickett's Division

Garnett's Brigade: 8th, 18th, 19th, 28th, 56th Virginia Infantry Regiments

Kemper's Brigade: 1st, 3rd, 7th, 11th, 24th Virginia Infantry Regiments

Armistead's Brigade: 9th, 14th, 38th, 53rd, 57th Virginia Infantry Regiments

Divisional Artillery: Companies A (Fauquier Artillery), B (Richmond Fayette Artillery), C (Hampden Artillery), D (Blount's Battery), 38th Virginia Artillery Battalion

Hood's Division

Law's Brigade: 4th, 15th, 44th, 47th, 48th Alabama Infantry Regiments

Robertson's Brigade: 3rd Arkansas, 1st, 4th, 5th Texas Infantry Regiments

Anderson's Brigade: 7th, 8th, 9th, 11th, 59th Georgia Infantry Regiments

Benning's Brigade: 2nd, 15th, 17th, 20th Georgia Infantry Regiments

Divisional Artillery: Branch Artillery (Co. H, 40th North Carolina); German (South Carolina) Artillery; Palmetto (South Carolina Artillery); Rowan Artillery (Co. D, 10th North Carolina)

FIFTH CORPS RESERVE ARTILLERY

Alexander's Battalion: Ashland (Virginia) Artillery; Bedford (Virginia) Artillery; Brooks (South Carolina) Artillery; Madison (Louisiana) Artillery; Parker (Virginia) Light Artillery; Co. C, 12th Virginia Artillery Battalion

Washington (Louisiana) Artillery Battalion: First, Second, Third, Fourth Companies

SECOND (EWELL'S) CORPS

Headquarters: Co. B, 39th Virginia Cavalry Battalion

Early's Division

Hays' Brigade: 5th, 6th, 7th, 8th, 9th Louisiana Infantry Regiments

Smith's Brigade: 31st, 49th, 52nd Virginia Infantry Regiments

Hoke's Brigade: 6th North Carolina State Troops, 21st, 57th North Carolina Infantry Regiments

Gordon's Brigade: 13th, 26th, 31st, 38th, 60th, 61st Georgia Infantry Regiments

Divisional Artillery: Charlottesville (Virginia) Artillery; Courtney (Virginia) Artillery; Louisiana Guard Artillery; Staunton (Virginia) Artillery

Johnson's Division

Steuart's Brigade: 2nd Maryland Infantry Battalion, 1st, 3rd North Carolina, 10th, 23rd, 37th Virginia Infantry Regiments

Stonewall Brigade: 2nd, 4th, 5th, 27th, 33rd Virginia Infantry Regiments

Nicholls' Brigade: 1st, 2nd, 10th, 14th, 15th Louisiana Infantry Regiments

Jones' Brigade: 21st, 25th, 42nd, 44th, 48th, 50th Virginia Infantry Regiments

Divisional Artillery: 1st, 4th (Chesapeake) Maryland Batteries; Alleghany (Virginia) Artillery; Lynchburg Lee (Virginia) Battery

Rodes' Division

Daniel's Brigade: 32nd, 43rd, 45th, 53rd North Carolina Infantry Regiments, 2nd North Carolina Infantry Brigade

Doles' Brigade: 4th, 12th, 21st, 44th Georgia Infantry Regiments

Iverson's Brigade: 5th North Carolina State Troops, 12th, 20th, 23rd North Carolina Infantry Regiments

Ramseur's Brigade: 2nd, 4th North Carolina State Troops, 14th, 30th North Carolina Infantry Regiments

O'Neal's Brigade: 3rd, 5th, 6th, 12th, 26th Alabama Infantry Regiments
Divisional Artillery: Jeff Davis (Alabama) Artillery; King William (Virginia) Artillery; Morris (Virginia) Artillery; Orange (Virginia) Artillery

SECOND CORPS ARTILLERY RESERVE

First Virginia Artillery: 2nd, 3rd Companies, Richmond Howitzers; Powhatan Artillery; First Rockbridge Artillery; Salem Flying Artillery
Nelson's Battalion: Co. A, 31st Virginia Artillery Battalion (Amherst Artillery); Fluvanna (Virginia) Artillery; Milledge's (Georgia) Battery

THIRD (HILL'S) CORPS

Anderson's Division
Wilcox's Brigade: 8th, 9th, 10th, 11th, 14th Alabama Infantry Regiments
Mahone's Brigade: 6th, 12th, 16th, 41st, 61st Virginia Infantry Regiments
Wright's Brigade: 3rd, 22nd, 48th Georgia Infantry Regiments, 2nd Georgia Infantry Battalion
Perry's Brigade: 2nd, 5th, 8th Florida Infantry Regiments
Posey's Brigade: 12th, 16th, 19th, 48th Mississippi Infantry Regiments
Divisional Artillery: Companies A, B, C, 11th Georgia (Sumter) Artillery Battalion

Heth's Division
First (Pettigrew's) Brigade: 11th, 26th, 47th, 52nd North Carolina Infantry Regiments
Second (Brockenbrough's) Brigade: 40th, 47th, 55th Virginia Infantry Regiments, 22nd Virginia Infantry Battalion
Third (Archer's) Brigade: 13th Alabama Infantry Regiment, 5th Alabama Infantry Battalion, 1st Tennessee (Provisional Army) Infantry Regiment, 7th, 14th Tennessee Infantry Regiments
Fourth (Davis') Brigade: 2nd, 11th, 42nd Mississippi, 55th North Carolina Infantry Regiments
Divisional Artillery: Donaldsonville (Louisiana) Artillery; Huger (Virginia) Artillery; Lewis (Virginia) Artillery; Norfolk (Virginia) Light Artillery Blues

Pender's Division
First (Perrin's) Brigade: 1st South Carolina (Provisional Army) Infantry Regiment, 1st South Carolina Rifles, 12th, 13th, 14th South Carolina Infantry Regiments
Second (Lane's) Brigade: 7th North Carolina State Troops, 18th, 28th, 33rd, 37th North Carolina Infantry Regiments
Third (Thomas') Brigade: 14th, 35th, 45th, 49th Georgia Infantry Regiments
Fourth (Scales') Brigade: 13th, 16th, 22nd, 34th, 38th North Carolina Infantry Regiments
Divisional Artillery: Albemarle Everett (Virginia) Artillery; Charlotte (Co. C, 10th North Carolina) Artillery; Madison (Mississippi) Light Artillery; Brooke (Virginia) Artillery

THIRD CORPS ARTILLERY RESERVE

McIntosh's Battalion: Danville (Virginia) Artillery; Hardaway (Alabama) Artillery; Second

Rockbridge (Virginia) Artillery; Johnson's/Cutter's (Virginia) Battery

Pegram's Battalion: Crenshaw (Virginia) Battery; Fredericksburg (Virginia) Artillery; Letcher (Virginia) Artillery; Pee Dee (South Carolina) Artillery; Purcell (Virginia) Artillery

Cavalry (Stuart's) Division

Hampton's Brigade: 1st North Carolina, 1st, 2nd South Carolina Cavalry Regiments, Cavalry of Cobb's (Georgia), Jeff Davis' (Mississippi), Phillip's (Georgia) Legions

Robertson's Brigade: 4th, 5th North Carolina Cavalry Regiments

Fitz Lee's Brigade: 1st, 2nd, 3rd, 4th, 5th Virginia Cavalry Regiments

Jenkins' Brigade: 8th, 14th, 16th, 17th Virginia Cavalry Regiments, 34th, 36th, 37th Virginia Cavalry Battalions, Kanawha (Virginia) Artillery

Jones' Brigade: 1st Maryland Cavalry Battalion, 6th, 7th, 11th, 12th Virginia Cavalry Regiments, 35th Virginia Cavalry Battalion

W. H. F. Lee's Brigade: 2nd North Carolina, 9th, 10th, 13th, 15th Virginia Cavalry Regiments

Stuart Horse Artillery: 1st Stuart (Virginia) Horse Artillery; Ashby (Virginia) Artillery; 2nd Maryland Light Artillery Battery; Washington (South Carolina) Artillery; McGregor's (Virginia) Battery; Lynchburg (Virginia) Beauregard's Artillery

Imboden's Command: 18th Virginia Cavalry Regiment, 62nd Virginia Mounted Infantry Regiment, McNeill's Virginia Partisan Rangers, McClanahan's (Virginia) Battery

3 WEAPONS AND EQUIPMENT

Essentially both sides used variations of the same types of weapons. The standard infantryman's arm was a single-shot, muzzle-loading, percussion-fired musket or rifle musket. The musket was smoothbore and fired a single lead ball and three buckshot; the rifle musket fired a special round known as the Minié ball after its French inventor. Most Federal soldiers carried muskets or rifle muskets made at the Springfield Armory, Massachusetts, or by various private manufacturers who produced weapons to US Ordnance Department standards under government contract.

The musket was either a US Army M1816 style or an M1842 style, which was produced starting in 1844. Both fired a 0.69-calibre ball with three buckshot and were considered obsolete weapons by the outset of the Civil War. As there were not enough of the latest model rifle muskets available, many of them came out of armouries to equip volunteer units. It had a triangular spike bayonet. Some 1842 muskets were later rifled with a long-range sight replacing the earlier simple sight. These fired a 0.69-calibre conical Minié ball.

By 1863 the Army of the Potomac's commanders could have replaced most of them with the later models, but many regimental commanders preferred the older smoothbores. At the typical fighting ranges of several hundred yards they estimated that the larger ammunition, with its scattering buckshot, would do more damage than the rifle musket. Among the defenders of the Federal line at Pickett's charge, for example, were the men of the 12th New Jersey, part of Smyth's Brigade in II Corps, armed with these smoothbores. Other regiments in the brigade were armed with rifle muskets and were therefore able to open fire on the advancing Confederates at greater ranges than the men of the 12th. The 12th were instructed to take cover behind the fence, then get up and fire when the lead Confederates were some 50 yards away. It was the belief of many in the 12th that the smoothbore ammunition helped stop the charge, which reached no more than a dozen yards from their position at best. Albert Stokes Emmell of the regiment said that the Confederate dead on their front looked like wheat sheaves laid out in lines.

According to *The Field Manual for The Use of the Officers on Ordnance Duty*, printed at Richmond in 1862, a musket ball fired with the standard charge would penetrate 10½ inches of seasoned white pine at 200 yards; 6⅓ inches at 600 yards; and 3½ inches at 1,000 yards. The weapon's muzzle velocity was 362 feet per second.

In 1841 the US Army began production of a percussion cap rifle, which was shorter than a musket, at its Harpers Ferry Armory, although a handful were also produced at the Springfield Armory. This fired a 0.54-calibre ball and it gained some fame in the Mexican War when Jefferson Davis' Mississippi Volunteers

Enfield Pattern 0.577-calibre Infantry Rifle-Musket.

used the weapon with great effectiveness at the Battle of Buena Vista. However, it was a heavy weapon and used an expensive sabre bayonet and not a great number were produced. At the outset of the Civil War many of these were rebored to accept a 0.58-calibre cartridge, but they saw limited use in the war and relatively few would have been seen at Gettysburg.

In 1855 the US Army adopted a new rifle musket that fired a 0.58-calibre Minié ball. It had an elaborate sight that could be set for as far as 900 yards, and a patented Maynard primer system that used a roll of paper caps. Every time the hammer was cocked, a new cap would be advanced from the mechanism on the lock. This system turned out to be less than wholly effective in wet weather, the damp getting between the two strips of paper that housed the fulminate of mercury which fired the round. A shorter rifle of this design was also adopted. While the rifle took a sabre bayonet, the rifle musket was equipped with a triangular spike bayonet.

In 1861, faced with the need to arm large numbers of men quickly, the Army produced the M1861 which was a simplified version of the M1855. The Maynard priming system was dropped in favour of the old separate copper percussion cap system used in the M1841 rifle, and the sight was simplified to a two-blade version; whereas many M1855 rifle muskets had a patchbox set into the butt, the M1861 model had no patchbox. Otherwise the two rifle muskets were quite similar. No M1861 rifles (as against rifle muskets) were produced. This, made by the Springfield Armory and a number of private manufacturers under contract, became the standard Union Army infantry firearm and made up the majority of the Federal infantry longarms on the field at Gettysburg. The men called these weapons, regardless of maker, 'Springfields'.

Production machinery for the M1855 rifle and rifle musket was captured on the destruction of the Harpers Ferry Armory by Virginia state forces in 1861. Rifle musket machinery went to the Confederate Richmond Armory, and rifle machinery to the Fayetteville, North Carolina, Armory. Copies of these weapons were thereafter made for Confederate forces and saw action at Gettysburg. Many more M1861 rifle muskets, however, were collected after the Army of Northern Virginia's successful actions at Manassas, Fredericksburg, and Chancellorsville.

According to the Confederate ordnance field manual, a rifle musket, with the standard charge of 60 grains of powder, had a muzzle velocity of 583 feet per second. It would penetrate 11 inches of seasoned white pine at 300 yards, 6⅓ inches at 600 yards, and 3½ inches at 1,000 yards. Moreover it was possible to hit the target at this extreme range, which was not the case with the smoothbore musket.

Both the Union and Confederate Armies also purchased large numbers of copies of the British P1858 rifle musket, a 0.577-calibre, percussion cap, muzzle-loading, single-shot weapon, known to American users as 'Enfields'. These were not, however, the product of the British Army's Enfield Armoury. Union copies were made largely by Birmingham gunmakers, while essentially the entire production of the London Armoury, a private concern, went South. This weapon became the standard Confederate longarm. It performed about the same as the M1855/M1861 rifle musket.

Some soldiers seem to have preferred the American-designed weapon to the Enfield. After their successful defence of Little Round Top on 2 July men of the 20th Maine Infantry found so many abandoned rifle muskets that they traded the Enfields with which they had been armed for the M1861 rifle muskets lying about. According to one of the regiment's members, the Enfields shot well enough, but were difficult to maintain and the men believed that it would halve the time to clean the M1861 rifle muskets. Although they called all these weapons 'Springfields', it is probable that some of them were Richmond-made copies of the weapon.

The Austrian Lorenz 0.54-calibre rifle musket was also imported by both sides in large quantities and was widely seen at Gettysburg. Other Austrian rifle muskets and muskets, as well as muskets and rifle muskets from German states, Belgium, and France were imported by both sides, but most were used by rear echelon troops by the time of Gettysburg and few would have been seen on that field.

FitzGerald Ross, an Austrian officer who visited Lee's army during the Gettysburg Campaign, later wrote: 'In Pennsylvania, Lee's army, with the exception of Hood's division [which seems to have had a large number of Austrian Lorenz rifle muskets in its ranks], was armed with Enfield and Springfield rifles.' Fremantle, who was with Lee's army at the same time as Ross, reported that, 'The Confederate troops are now entirely armed with excellent rifles, mostly Enfields.'

Some Federal troops were armed with breech-loading longarms. The 0.52-calibre Sharps rifle was a single-shot weapon whose paper-wrapped cartridge was loaded through a falling breechblock. It had a ladder-type sight graduated from 100 to 800 yards. These weapons not only had a faster rate of fire than the three shots a minute of the muzzle-loading rifle muskets, but could be fired from a prone or kneeling position without the soldier having to get up to reload. They were in use by the 1st and 2nd US Sharpshooters as well as the 1st Company, Massachusetts Sharpshooters, and some men of the 1st Minnesota, the 14th Connecticut, and the 2nd New Hampshire.

The ammunition was carried in a leather case, called the cartridge box, which featured a heavy outer and a thinner inner flap. American-made boxes held 40 rounds in tin containers, but some Confederates had British-made boxes that held 50 rounds. All the British boxes were slung on shoulder belts from the left shoulder to the right hip. US Army issue boxes could either be carried on a similar belt, with a circular brass plate worn on the centre of the chest, or on the waistbelt. Officials strongly preferred the men to wear them on the shoulder belt, although some men discarded these belts and wore them on the waistbelt. Many Southern-made boxes had straps for waistbelt use only.

A smaller leather percussion cap box was worn on the waistbelt on the right front hip, and the bayonet scabbard hung from the waistbelt on the left side. Generally the men had a cotton haversack, slung from the right shoulder over the bayonet scabbard; in the US army most were rainproofed by a black coating. Rations and another 20 rounds of ammunition were carried in the haversack. A tin canteen hung from the right shoulder over the top of the haversack. Because of raw material scarcities in the South, many Confederate troops had wooden canteens, like little casks, instead of tin ones. Generally, however, Confederate infantrymen were able to obtain superior Northern-made equipment on the battlefield, and exchanged their Southern-made haversacks and canteens for Union models.

Federal troops were issued with a black-painted knapsack, which was worn in the centre of the man's back, unit identification being marked in white. The brown issue army blanket was stored in the middle of this, while a sky-blue overcoat was strapped to the top of the knapsack. Shoulder-straps passed under a narrow wooden rod on top to keep the knapsack snug to the top of the back. A wide variety of bag knapsacks, as well as imported copies of British Army knapsacks, were issued in the Confederate Army. Many men simply picked up a discarded Federal knapsack on the battlefield. Fremantle later noted that, 'The knapsacks of the men still bear the names of the Massachusetts, Vermont, New Jersey, or other regiments to which they originally belonged.' The majority of Confederates, however, simply wrapped up whatever spare clothing they had in their blanket and wore it, horseshoe style, over a shoulder. Fremantle noted that in Hood's Division the men 'carry less than any other troops; many of them have only got an old piece of carpet or rug as baggage ...' This, combined with grey clothing that faded into various shades of brown, gave the Confederates rather a ragamuffin appearance, something Fremantle admired: 'Now, the Confederate has no ambition to imitate the regular soldier at all. He looks the genuine Rebel; but in spite of his bare feet, his ragged clothes, his old rug, and toothbrush stuck like a rose in his buttonhole (This tooth-brush in the buttonhole is a very common custom, and has a most quaint effect), he has a sort of devil-may-care, reckless, self-confident look, which is decidedly taking.'

Officers carried a sword slung from a swordbelt on the left hip, and often a pistol in a black leather holster on the right. The pistol was quite often a Colt 0.36-calibre Navy revolver, although many other types, being privately purchased and not according to any regulation, were also seen. Officers usually purchased fancier, larger haversacks than the men, made with different compartments inside and often with impressed insignia on the flap. They also managed to 'find' issue canteens.

Artillery officers had the same equipment as the infantry officers. The men, however, were only issued with haversacks and canteens and, in the Union Army, swordbelts and copies of a French Army light artillery sabre. These were generally left behind or in a battery wagon in the field. One man in each gun crew had a large brown leather haversack that was used to carry ammunition from the limber chest to the gun; another man would have a small brown leather case on a brown waistbelt containing fuses for the ammunition.

For the most part, three types of cannon accompanied the armies. The M1857 'Napoleon' smoothbore 12pdr gun, with a bronze barrel, was adopted by the US Army prior to the war and was used widely by both sides. According to Ross, 'The field-piece most generally employed is the smooth-bored 12-pound "Napoleon" (*canon obusier*), which fires solid shot, shell, case, and canister: it is much lighter than the ordinary 12-pounder [howitzer], and they can give it an elevation of nine to ten degrees.' It fired solid shot at distances ranging between 325 to 1,680 yards, the latter at 3.45 degrees of elevation.

Lee's artillery also included a number of bronze 12- and 24pdr smoothbore howitzers. The 12pdr was the model replaced by the Napoleon in the US Army, and these weapons were not in field use in that force. However, 'In Northern Virginia 12-pound howitzers and 6-pounder guns are discarded, and Napoleons have been cast from their metal; here there are still a large number, and a few 24-pounder howitzers. Colonel [E. Porter] Alexander thinks highly of these last', Ross wrote. The 12pdr could fire a solid shot from 195 to 1,072 yards, the latter at five degrees of elevation. The 24pdr had a range between 295 and 1,322 yards.

At Gettysburg the Army of the Potomac's artillery park was made up of 40 per cent smoothbore guns; The Army of Northern Virginia's artillery park was virtually half and half, smoothbore and rifled guns. Cost played a part in the decision by the US Ordnance Department to provide so many rifled guns. A bronze Napoleon cost some $440, while an iron Parrott rifle cost $350 and a 3in Ordnance rifle cost $380.

'Then there are the 10 and 20 pound Parrotts ...,' Ross wrote. These rifled weapons, marked by having a band of iron wrapped around their breech during the manufacturing process for added strength, were manufactured in the North at the West Point Armory, a private concern, to the design of Army officer Robert Parrott. 'They are rifled guns, with a wrought-iron band at the breach; their bore is 2.90. Those in this army are chiefly captured from the Yankees, but some are made at the Tredegar Works at Richmond; they throw solid bolts, shell, case, and canister.' Maximum range of the 10pdr Parrott was 1,850 yards at five degrees.

The Parrott was widely used in both armies, the 20pdr version being the largest piece of field artillery available. But it was prone to explode prematurely while in use, and the greater the bore diameter, the more vulnerable was the piece. Nor was it considered a successful weapon; its great weight made it slow to move, but on the other hand it was not heavy enough for proper siege use.

'The 3-inch rifled gun [3-inch Ordnance rifle] is very similar; and the best of these, too, are taken from the enemy.' The 3in Ordnance rifle was produced by the Phoenixville Iron Works, Phoenixville, Pennsylvania, to a unique design. Its smooth, bottle-shape design made it a lighter tube than the other types. Only one out of 1,100 Northern-made Ordnance rifles ever exploded prematurely while being used, while the explosion rate for Southern-made copies was only slightly worse. At Gettysburg a Southern-made Ordnance rifle in Reilly's Battery burst in the evening of 2 July while in support of Hood's attack on Devil's Den and Little Round Top. Maximum range of the Ordnance rifle at five degrees was 1,830 yards.

Lee's artillery arsenal also included a battery of Austrian bronze, smoothbore howitzers with a calibre of 5.87in, and two extremely accurate, steel breech-loading, British-made Whitworth rifles. Ross noted that these latter were, 'very accurate and of great range, but require much care. The breech has sometimes been blown off or disabled in loading. This was especially the case with breech-loading guns ... Their field-ammunition the Confederates consider to be far superior to that of the Yankees.' The Whitworths saw very little use in the Gettysburg campaign. Their carriages appear to have been too delicate for rough field use, and had to be replaced by new ones made in Richmond. The weapons were accurate at such long ranges, up to five miles, that the period had no range-finding devices or way of indirect fire control that could take advantage of them. Moreover, the Confederate ordnance manufacturers were unable to duplicate accurately the ammunition made in England for these guns, so their expensive ammunition had to be brought in through the blockade. Thus artillery officers limited the use of their Whitworths to only obvious targets where the gunners could easily see their targets, such as when the Federals were retreating from Fredericksburg.

The Whitworth was also equipped with a special deflector shield that protected its gunners from friction primers that were blown backward on firing like a bullet, having the potential to cause injury among the crew.

Confederate horse artillery also used four British-made, iron, Blakely guns, described by artillery Colonel E. P. Alexander as, 'twelve pounder rifles, muzzle-loaders, and fired well with English ammunition ("built up" shells with leaden bases), but with the Confederate substitute, they experienced the same difficulties which attended this ammunition in all guns. The only advantage to be claimed for this gun is its lightness, but this was found to involve the very serious evil that no field carriage could be made to withstand its recoil. It was continually splitting the trails or racking to pieces its carriages, though made of unusual strength and weight.'

One 4-gun Union battery was armed with a bronze rifled 12pdr cannon, the James rifle. This was a poor weapon, however, in that the bronze rifling wore down quickly and accuracy after any use was little better than that of the Napoleon.

Fremantle echoed Ross when he noted that among the cannon in Lee's army, the majority 'bear the letters US, showing that they have changed masters'. Fremantle also noted that in the Confederate Army, 'The artillery horses are in poor condition and only get 3 lb. of corn a day.'

Confederate artillerymen were at a disadvantage compared to their Union counterparts in that primers, fuses, and ammunition made by Southern manufacturers were of poor quality. So many shells exploded prematurely that Confederate infantry rarely allowed their artillery to fire over their heads, fearful of these 'friendly fire' explosions in their own ranks.

Cavalrymen on both sides were armed with revolver, sabre and carbine. Neither government produced revolvers at its own plants, but bought them from private manufacturers. The revolver mostly used by both sides was a Colt design. The standard Union cavalry revolver was a 0.44-calibre Colt 'Army', which held six shots in a cylinder that revolved when cocked. Many officers preferred the M1851 Colt 0.36-calibre Colt 'Navy' model and acquired them privately. Southern manufacturers such as Leech & Rigdon and Griswold and Gunnison made copies of the Colt Navy revolver which they sold to both the central Confederate

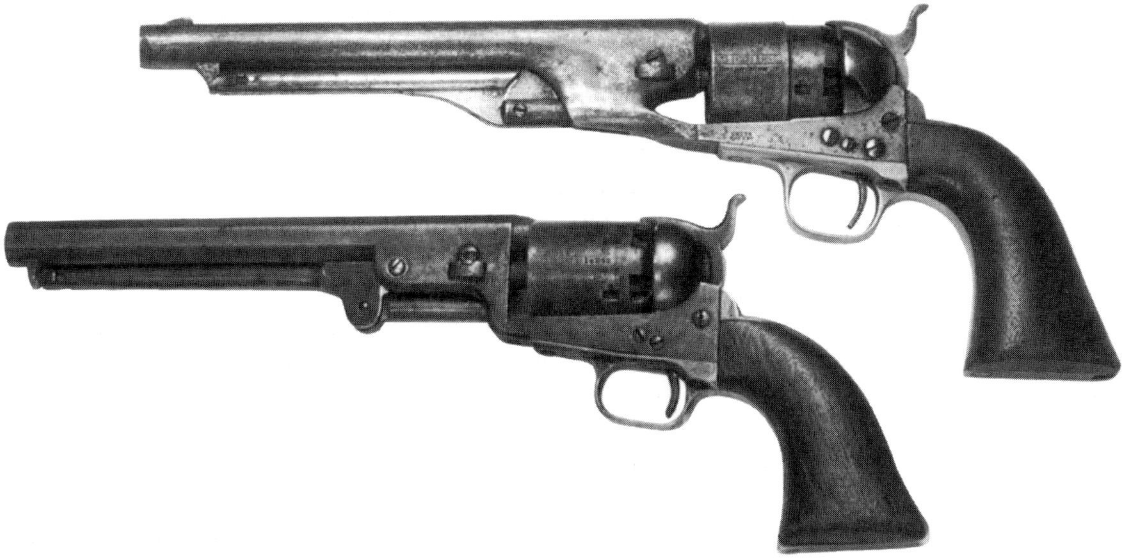

A 0.44-calibre Colt Army Model 1860 and below it a 0.36-calibre Model 1851 Navy.

government or state governments. Southern-made 'Colts' used inferior materials and were of noticeably poorer quality than the Northern made examples.

The Remington Army revolver was a close second to the Colt in Union cavalry use, as were its Navy models. These were stronger than the Colts because they featured a top-strap over the cylinder. Moreover, the ease with which the cylinder could be removed made them faster to reload. Southern manufacturers, however, did not copy Remington revolvers. In all, the US Ordnance Department purchased revolvers from fourteen manufacturers, each with its unique design. These included the Adams, a British-made revolver which was popular with officers, and a French-made pin-fire revolver, the Le Faucheux, which was unpopular and saw little use in the Army of the Potomac. All came in 0.44in Army or 0.36in Navy calibre. As with longarms, a large proportion of the Army of Northern Virginia cavalry revolvers were acquired on the battlefield.

Revolvers were carried in a black leather holster worn on the swordbelt. The sabre was hung on the left side from the same belt.

The standard US cavalry sabre was a Northern-made copy of a French cavalry sabre, either the M1840 heavy cavalry sabre or the lighter M1860 version. Both had a slightly curved blade with a single blood gutter, a brass hilt, and a black leather handgrip held in place by twisted brass wire. The scabbard was polished iron, sometimes blackened for protection against rust, and a brown leather sabre knot was passed over the wrist and around the hilt so that the weapon would not be lost in horseback action.

The Confederate government obtained Southern-made copies of these sabres, but again using poorer quality materials such as oilcloth in place of leather for the grips, brass for the iron scabbards, and poor quality steel for the blades. In fact, however, this mattered little to members of the Army of Northern Virginia's cavalry for, as Fremantle wrote, 'they wear swords, but seem to have little idea of using them – they hanker after their carbines and revolvers. They constantly ride with their swords between their left leg and the saddle, which has a very funny appearance; but their horses are generally good, and they ride well.' Later he noted that, 'Neither party has any idea of serious charging with the sabre. They approach one another with considerable boldness, until they get to within about forty yards, and then, at the very moment when a dash is necessary, and the sword alone should be used, they hesitate, halt, and commence a desultory fire with carbines and revolvers.' In fact, however, generally Union cavalry brigade commanders organised one or two cavalry regiments as 'sabre regiments', trained in the use of the sabre, while the others specialised more in dismounted service using their carbines.

Carbines, at least in the Union Army, as pistols, were manufactured by private concerns with different patent versions. The usual Union carbine was a single-shot, breech-loader, ranging in calibre between 0.50in and 0.52in. The Sharps carbine was the most common of these. It used a 0.52in calibre paper- or linen-wrapped cartridge which was consumed when it was fired. It was loaded from behind a falling breech-block. Other types of cartridge also saw use; for example, the Burnside used a brass cartridge and the Smith used a foil or rubber cartridge. The same principle of having an opening in the breech into which the cartridge was placed was used by all these single-shot carbines.

In March 1863 the Confederate Army began issuing copies of the Sharps carbine made in Richmond by a private manufacturer. The first copies earned a bad reputation among Army of Northern Virginia cavalrymen for bursting at the breech upon firing. The problem seems to have been the inability of the manufacturer, whose plant was soon taken over by the Confederate government, to work to the close tolerances demanded by the Sharps Company's plant. Nevertheless the weapons were manufactured almost to the end of the war, some 5,000 of them having been produced and issued, mostly in the Army of Northern Virginia.

Some private manufacturers elsewhere in the South also produced carbines in small numbers, some using brass cartridges that were very difficult to manufacture because of the lack of materials. But these accounted for a small proportion of the total cavalry armoury. Most Confederate cavalrymen carried short versions of the 0.58-calibre Richmond rifle musket or the 0.577 'Enfield' British- and Southern-made rifle musket. Eventually, some time after Gettysburg, the 0.577 muzzle-loading Enfield carbine was selected as the standard Confederate carbine.

This difference in firepower between the Union cavalry's breech-loading carbines and the Confederates' muzzle-loaders was a significant factor when estimating the potential firepower of the two sides; on horseback the muzzle-loader was much more awkward to load than a breech-loader.

Carbines were carried slung on a wide leather belt worn from the right shoulder to the left side. Cavalrymen also carried the issue haversack and canteen, and most carried a second canteen for the horse, slung from the saddle.

4

THE BATTLE

1 JULY

At about noon on 30 June a division of Union cavalry, three brigades strong, under Brigadier General John Buford, entered the small cross-roads town of Gettysburg, Pennsylvania. Like the spokes of a wheel, roads extended out from the town's centre west to Chambersburg, north to Carlisle, east to York, and south to Baltimore. Buford's men rode in along the Emmitsburg Road, coming north from the Maryland line, then turned to ride through the town along Washington Street. Inhabitants lined the town's sidewalks to cheer their tired and dirty saviours.

Buford had headed towards Gettysburg with a purpose. His advance units had picked up a number of Confederate stragglers who provided him with excellent intelligence on the enemy. At 5.30 on the 30th, while still on the way towards Gettysburg, Buford was able to send a message back to both John Reynolds and Alfred Pleasonton that he'd been able to determine that the Confederates were in strength towards Cashtown, to the west, while more were 'toward Mummasburg'. He also advised his two superiors of a cavalry battle at Hanover. His later messages reported that Hill's Corps was at Cashtown, and Ewell's Corps was coming that way from Carlisle, while rumour had it that another force was coming towards Gettysburg from York. But Buford's horsemen had beaten them all to Gettysburg.

On the western edge of the town was a Lutheran seminary, on the Chambersburg Pike. It was a tall brick building with a white cupola from where one could view, in fair weather, the gently rolling countryside for miles. Buford halted his men in the seminary grounds, camping on the western side of Seminary Ridge while sending several squadrons forward as a picket line. That evening he told one of his brigade commanders that the next morning he expected that, 'They will attack you in the morning and will come "booming", skirmishers three deep. You will have to fight like the devil to hold your own until supports arrive. The enemy must know the importance of this position, and will strain every nerve to secure it, and if we are able to hold it we shall do well.'

At about 5 o'clock next morning the Confederate division commanded by Major General Henry Heth, of Hill's Corps, broke its rough camp in the Cashtown area and headed towards Gettysburg. The men knew that other Confederates had passed through Gettysburg earlier with no opposition and did not anticipate finding any blue troops there that day. A light rain began to fall as the lead troops reached the swampy Marsh Creek floodplain and first saw, across the fields, dismounted Federal cavalrymen holding their horses. The Confederate regiments halted and began to deploy from a 4-man column into 2-man deep battle lines. Heth's artillery battalion commander also spotted the Federals and halted, unlimbering one of its 3in Ordnance rifles and running it forward.

At about 7 o'clock, pickets from the 8th Illinois Cavalry spotted the advancing Confederates. One of them, Lieutenant Marcellus E. Jones, borrowed a carbine from one of his sergeants, Levi S. Shafer and, at about half-past seven, rested the weapon on a rail fence and fired at a Confederate on a grey horse just left of the familiar red Army of Northern Virginia battle flag. The battle had begun.

The lead brigade, commanded by James Archer, sent out skirmishers from the 5th Alabama Battalion, the 13th Alabama Regiment, and the 1st Tennessee, on the south side of the Chambersburg Pike (now Route 30). Another skirmish line from the 55th North Carolina advanced along the north side of the road. The colour-bearer of the 13th Tennessee uncased his colour, previously wrapped in oilskin to protect it from the light rain, and prepared to advance behind the skirmish line. Major William Pegram, Heth's artillery commander, had his gun open fire, but after only several shots had it limbered up to advance. This shot was probably the first fired from the Confederate side in the battle.

The first casualty of the battle seems to have been the canine mascot of Co. A, 5th Alabama Battalion, hit by a shot from the first volley from the cavalry carbines. Men from the 13th Alabama had revenge of a sort by shooting an annoying, barking dog owned by a farmer whose land they crossed. The first Confederate human casualty was Private C. L. F. Worley, Co. A, 5th Alabama Battalion, who lost a leg as a result of his wound; the first Union casualty was an unknown cavalryman who was among the reinforcements riding up and, in the lead on a white horse, was shot before he could dismount.

The Federal cavalrymen fell back slowly, firing as they did. The firing alerted the rest of Co. E of the 8th Illinois, who came up to the aid of their hard-pressed pickets. The company commander posted his men as a very open order line, some 30 feet between one another, and had them begin fire at 800 yards, an extreme range for carbines, which were quite inaccurate at such ranges. The Confederate line was longer than the Federal line, open as it was, armed with better weapons for such long-range fighting, and stronger in numbers. Although other elements of the forward Federal lines joined the fight, the cavalry was weakened by 25 per cent since for every four men fighting, one was detached to the rear to hold his and the other three horses. The result was that about 150 Union cavalrymen armed with short-range carbines were being pressed by some 500 Confederate infantrymen armed with rifle muskets. The Federals slowly fell back towards a higher point, Herr Ridge.

However, for the Confederate infantry, some 1,200 officers and men in Archer's Brigade, deployment from column into line, and then breaking out of a skirmish line, while artillery unlimbered, took time. But after about an hour the Confederates had pressed the Federals back to the western slope of Herr Ridge. There they were joined by some 300 men from the 8th Illinois and 8th New York Cavalry Regiments, while Battery A, 2nd US Artillery, an all-mounted unit, unlimbered its guns on a small ridge overlooking Willoughby Run, on the road to Herr

Ridge. They faced a 2-gun section of 10pdr Parrott rifles from the Fredericksburg (Virginia) Artillery.

Archer's Brigade began to push forward, towards McPherson Woods, followed by Davis' Brigade on its left. The Federal cavalry, knowing that they had to hold on until their infantry could arrive on the field, fought with determination, but overwhelming numbers told. They slowly fell back, buying precious time.

That morning Major General John Reynolds, sleeping on a tavern floor seven miles south of Gettysburg, was woken by a courier with an order from Meade to move I and XI Corps to Gettysburg. Reynolds ordered the corps up and out, although without any urgency since he did not know of Heth's advance on that town. Then he headed towards the town himself. Some three miles south of Gettysburg he received word of Buford's engagement. Sending word back to hurry the infantry up, he quickly rode into Gettysburg, reaching the field just in time to see Archer's and Davis' Brigades deploying. Reynolds apparently liked the ground on which Buford had chosen to fight, and sent word back to Meade that he was going to give battle there. Then he went back to direct the arriving units towards the action.

Just as the cavalry line was collapsing, the infantry arrived, led by the 79th New York. Federal infantry deployed into line quickly, with the renowned Iron Brigade, the only western troops in the army, moving to block a threat to the Federal left. Their objective, pointed out by Reynolds, was Archer's Brigade, which had reached the Spring Hotel Woods and was headed towards the McPherson Woods. Without pausing, the Iron Brigade men fixed bayonets and dashed into the woods. But in the action, a stray round hit Reynolds in the neck at the back of his skull and he fell from his horse, dead.

On the Union right Cutler's Brigade formed a line, two regiments on one side of the Chambersburg Pike and an unfinished railroad cut that ran parallel to it, and three regiments on the other side. Davis' Brigade moved straight at it, sending one regiment to flank the right-hand regiment. That regiment, the 76th New York, moved to counter this attack, but could not hold, and the two right-hand regiments fell back towards Sheads' Woods. Somehow the third regiment did not get the word. Cut off, only 75 officers and men of the 147th managed to retreat in time, rallying behind Oak Ridge in line with the 76th New York and 56th Pennsylvania Regiments. An artillery battery posted between the railroad cut and the pike also had to limber up and take off under fire, losing a gun in the hasty retreat.

On the left, however, things were going better for the Federals. The Iron Brigade, following Reynolds' last orders, charged into the McPherson Woods, then occupied by the men of Archer's Brigade. Despite heavy losses, the westerners drove the Confederates out of the woods, capturing James Archer and killing or wounding about a third of his men. Archer became the first general of the Army of Northern Virginia to be captured in action.

Having cleared the woods, men of the Iron Brigade then turned to their right, from where they came under some fire, and assaulted units of Davis' Brigade

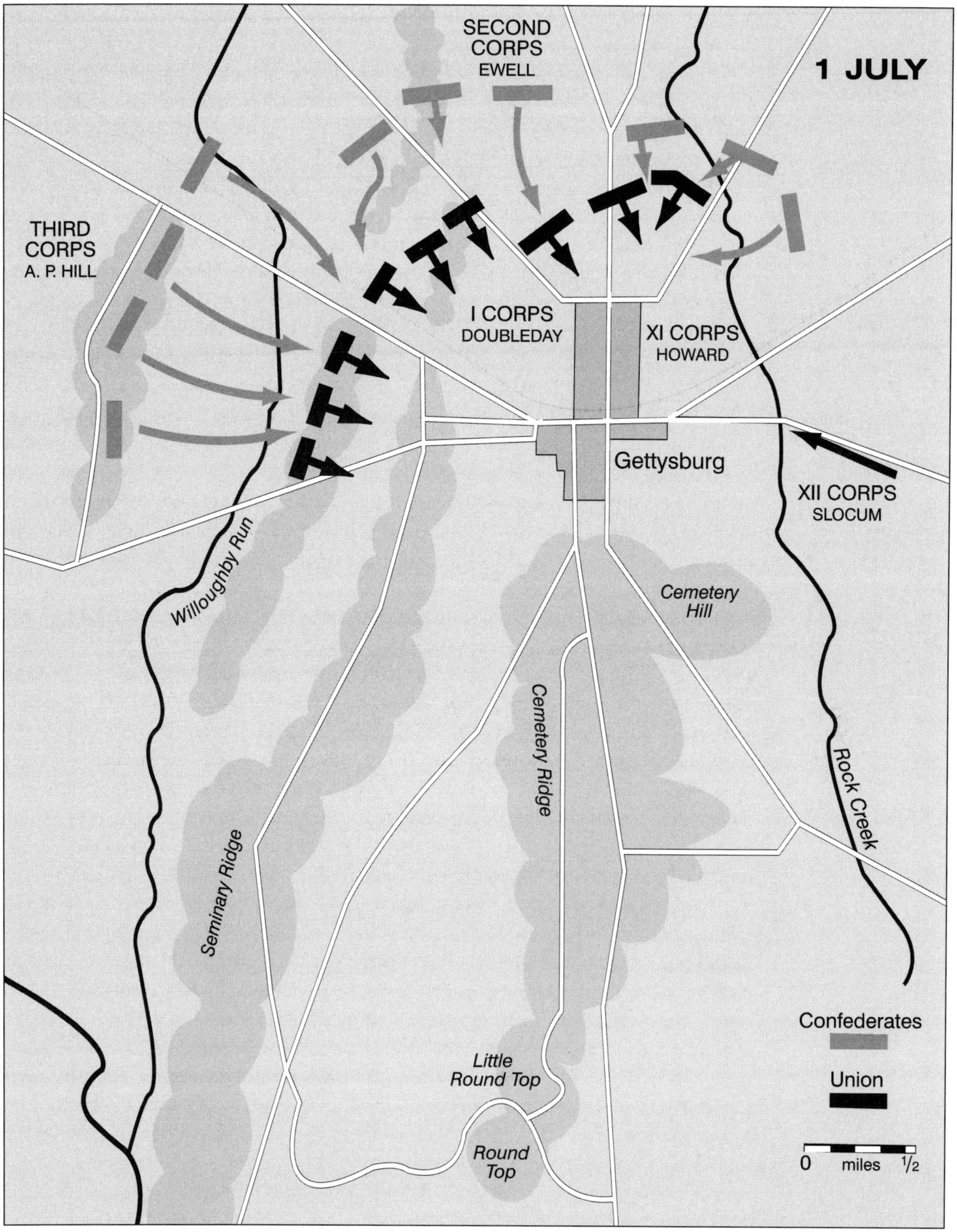
SECOND
CORPS
EWELL
1 JULY
THIRD
CORPS
A. P. HILL
I CORPS
DOUBLEDAY
XI CORPS
HOWARD
Gettysburg
XII CORPS
SLOCUM
Willoughby Run
Cemetery
Hill
Cemetery Ridge
Rock Creek
Seminary Ridge
Little
Round Top
Round
Top
Confederates
Union
0 miles 1/2

that had taken cover in the unfinished railroad cut and were firing on them. Joined by several New York regiments, the Federals captured the colour of the 2nd Mississippi along with hundreds of Confederates who had been trapped in the cut. With that, both sides drew back to find water, and fighting died down towards noon.

Before the sound of gunfire diminished, its noise had reached Cashtown, rousing A. P. Hill from his sickbed and attracting the attention of Lee, who wanted to avoid a battle at least until Stuart's cavalry, out there somewhere, could bring him hard intelligence of the situation. Hill had to admit that he had no idea what the gunfire signified and rode towards Gettysburg to find out, Lee slowly following. When Hill reached the field it appeared that his troops there had attacked and driven Federal cavalry and infantry back and a full fight seemed unavoidable. Hill ordered his full division deployed to follow up on the initial success.

Across the field, the Iron Brigade returned to defensive positions on the edge of McPherson Woods, while Cutler's Brigade moved back to its original positions. More I Corps Federal infantry reached the field and began to deploy in line with the units already there. Major General O. O. Howard, who after Reynolds' death was the senior officer on the field, reached the town and after looking around decided that Cemetery Hill was the best defensive position. Howard's own XI Corps began to arrive in the town at about 12.30. Dashing through the town at the double, the troops moved towards the right of I Corps. Howard went with them initially, then returned to Cemetery Hill where he set up his headquarters. From there he sent word to XII Corps, advising its commander of the situation in Gettysburg.

Initially John Slocum, the XII Corps commander, did not understand the importance of this message, only later learning of the seriousness of the fight from a civilian. But after a second message from Howard arrived at about 3 o'clock, he began moving to a position on the right of the Union line. An hour later Howard ordered the Federal troops to fall back towards Cemetery Hill if they couldn't hold any longer.

In the meantime troops from Ewell's Corps had begun to arrive on the field from the north, down the Harrisburg Road, in the centre of and flanking the right of the Union line. In the centre the division commanded by Major General Robert Rodes deployed into line on Oak Hill, its artillery forcing several Union units to change front to the north to meet this new threat. At about 2.30 Rodes attacked down the Oak Ridge towards the Mummasburg Road, his four regiments in a staggered line, with a wide gap between the one on the left flank and the one in the centre. His uncoordinated attack, although made with almost twice as many men as the Federals, failed, and his men fell back with heavy losses. As the Confederates fell back, Union defenders swarmed forward, capturing some 1,000 men and three colours. Rodes rallied the survivors for another try.

On the Federal right flank, Francis Barlow found that the ground he had been ordered to defend was level with only a slight rise along Stevens' Creek and offered little defensive advantage. Seeing a higher spot of ground, some 400 feet high, called Blocher's Knoll, to his front, he advanced his men to a position around that ground. The result was that his command was in advance of the rest of the Union line and somewhat isolated, though Barlow's superior in the area did not notice this until later when he gave orders to adjust the rest of the line on Barlow, but it was too late. Early's artillery opened fire, covering the area with shell and shot. Barlow himself sent reinforcements, apparently intending to hold the knoll, now known as Barlow's Knoll.

Early surveyed the situation and decided to disobey Lee's orders by ordering a full-scale assault, which was bound to bring about a general battle. In fact, however, Lee himself arrived on the field at about this time, and changed his mind about his earlier orders, allowing the attack, which he watched from Herr Ridge. At about 3.30 Early struck, just as Rodes was attacking again. His attack, led by Daniels' Brigade, stalled, and had to reform and attack three times. However, by his last attack, Major General John B. Gordon's brigade hit Barlow's exposed position. As his men fled, Barlow rode forward to rally them, but was shot in the left side of his body and fell from his horse. Picked up by Confederates, he was brought back to a hospital where eventually he recovered. Years later Gordon claimed that he himself aided Barlow, but his story appears to have been a fabrication.

Barlow's position having fallen, and his men now dashing towards the rear through the streets of Gettysburg, Confederates could now turn and fire on the rest of the Federal line. In only a matter of minutes the next brigade collapsed, and Federal artillery began to limber up and pull out. Some Federals fell back slowly, stopping to fire at the Confederates. One plucky colour-bearer was seen stopping from time to time to shake a fist at the grey line.

By the time Gordon's men had reached the almshouse on the Harrisburg Road, almost halfway between Barlow's Knoll and Gettysburg, its losses had been significant enough to diminish its fighting ability. Early decided to halt it there, sending another line forward to take its place. Federal commanders attempted to reform their units in the almshouse area, but Gordon's men were flushed with victory and soon drove them back towards the town.

At about 3:30 Howard sent forward Colonel Charles Coster's brigade, Second Division, XI Corps, which he had been holding on Cemetery Hill as a reserve. When they emerged from the town, Confederate artillery opened fire on them, and they drew into line around a brickyard. As the Confederates pressed forward, Coster was able to hang on only a short time before being forced to give the order to retreat. The men fled down streets and through back yards, many being captured in the rout. Some remained in the brickyard to fight hand-to-hand with the victorious Confederates. In all, when the smoke cleared, hundreds of Federals, both wounded and able-bodied, were in Confederate hands. The XI Corps, blamed for the defeat at Chancellorsville, had been routed again.

On the Federal left at 2.30, Heth again moved against I Corps troops on McPherson's Ridge. The Federal line there, including the Iron Brigade, had been badly bloodied in the morning's fighting, and much of the artillery had been withdrawn. Confederate artillery continued to fire before Heth's attack, causing more casualties. The fresh units that Heth sent forward faced fierce fighting, but by 2.40 the Federal I Corps' left flank began to collapse under pressure from North Carolina infantrymen. The Federals fell back towards Seminary Ridge, the Iron Brigade, which made the stiffest stand, falling back last. One of the men wounded with this unit was John Burns, a local civilian, a veteran of the War of 1812, who had taken the field to defend his town, wearing an old-fashioned blue swallowtail coat. Heth himself was wounded in the fight against these westerners, a stray shot hitting him in the head, serious injury being prevented by the paper stuffing he had put behind the hatband to make his large, newly found, hat fit.

The Federals reformed their line on Seminary Ridge while the Confederates reformed in the field facing them, using Pender's fresh division of Hill's Corps to replace Heth's battered troops. The Federal line was weak and lacked sufficient artillery support. Then, at about 4.30, the Confederates renewed their attack on the Federals. The Federal line was rolled up from its left, and had to abandon the position. Now fleeing I Corps men joined those of XI Corps escaping through Gettysburg, although some units managed to stage an orderly withdrawal.

At this time Lee and Hill, who was unwell, met to discuss attacking Cemetery Hill with the Third Corps. Hill said that his troops were exhausted in the weather that had turned hot and sunny after the early morning showers. Moreover, his

The Confederates of Heth's Division attacked from the tree line in the distance across the field to this point, which was defended by men of the 6th New York Cavalry on the morning of 1 July.

commands were disorganised and would take time to reform. Lee, who rarely pressed his generals to do anything they didn't want to do, accepted this without demur, although Hill, in fact, did have fresh troops available.

The advancing Confederates swiftly took over the town and the number of hospitals that had been set up in its public buildings and even private homes. In the fighting so far I Corps had lost about half its men; XI Corps had lost 41 per cent. The Iron Brigade had sustained losses of 73.2 per cent. Confederate losses, especially in officers of all ranks, had also been heavy, at about 25 per cent of their total, or 4,800 officers and men.

Howard himself met the retreating Federals, personally planting regimental colours in places on Cemetery Hill where he wanted the troops to reform, and instructing officers where to place their brigades. When Major General Abner Doubleday, temporary I Corps commander, reached Cemetery Hill Howard ordered him to post I Corps on the left of the cemetery, while he attended to XI Corps on the right. This he did, although he found his regiments greatly diminished by casualties and men who had simply gone missing. Some of the men who reformed there took delight in a sign posted at the cemetery gate: 'All persons found using firearms in these grounds will be prosecuted with the utmost rigor of the law.'

Confusion slowly gave way to steadied resolve. Brigadier General Thomas Rowley, who had taken over command of Doubleday's division when Doubleday moved to corps command on Reynolds' death, was found to be drunk and incoherent, and the corps provost marshal placed him under arrest. I Corps' artillery

chief, Colonel Charles Wainwright, managed to get 23 cannon in position on East Cemetery Hill, most of them facing Early's troops to the north-east. On the other side, twenty cannon were in position to cover the north-west side of Cemetery Hill. Survivors of Buford's cavalry moved to the left of Cemetery Hill where they threatened the Confederate right.

At about 4.30 Major General Winfield Scott Hancock, II Corps commander, named by Meade to command on the field in his absence, arrived. Before he left for the field his corps was given to Brigadier General John Gibbon to bring up to Gettysburg, while Hancock rode ahead. Meade also told Major General John Newton to replace Doubleday as I Corps commander and take over corps command from Howard. Hancock found Howard on Cemetery Hill and rode up to him with news of his change of command. What was actually said by the two at this meeting is unknown, but Howard, who ranked Hancock, could not have been pleased with this change of command. Indeed what actually happened there became a controversy that lasted throughout the two men's lives. Whatever happened, the result was that Howard went to direct operations on East Cemetery Hill, while Hancock concentrated on the right flank, deploying artillery and infantry to resist a further attack.

By 5 o'clock the Union position was fairly stable in a formidable defensive line. Hancock was able to report to Meade: 'We have now taken up a position in the cemetery, and cannot well be taken. It is a position, however, easily turned. Slocum (XII Corps) is now coming on the ground, and is taking position on the right, which will protect the right. But we have as yet no troops on the left, the Third Corps not having yet reported; but I suppose that it is marching up. If so, its flank march will in a degree protect our left flank. In the meantime Gibbon had better march on so as to take position on our right or left, to our rear, as may be necessary in some commanding position ... The battle is quiet now. I think we will be all right until night. I have sent all the trains back. When night comes, it can be told better what had best be done. I think we can retire; if not, we can fight here, as the ground appears not unfavorable with good troops.'

At about 6 o'clock Slocum's forces began to arrive in the area, as did lead elements of III Corps. Hancock prepared to turn over command to Slocum, who ranked him. Slocum, however, stayed with his corps, which later went into camp at Two Taverns. At about this time too, Meade sent word that VI Corps was coming up and he thought that the army should stay at Gettysburg and attack the Confederates there next day, being able to defeat the Army of Northern Virginia in detail. Meade also sent word to V Corps at about 7 o'clock to march to Gettysburg as quickly as possible.

Seeing the Federal lines beginning to harden, Lee sent word to Ewell at about 4.45, suggesting that his troops push forward and take Cemetery Hill. According to Colonel Walter Taylor, a staff officer who brought the message to Ewell, Lee said that the enemy was retreating in great confusion and 'it was only necessary to press "those people" in order to secure possession of the heights, and that, if possible [another version says 'practicable'], he wished him to do this.' Ewell, making his debut as a corps commander, rode with two of his divisional commanders from his headquarters in the town square down Baltimore Street and then the High Street to examine the Federal position. Aware that not all his troops were yet on the field and that those who were had been weakened by the day's fighting, and concerned by poor positions for his artillery, he did not find it 'practicable'. Instead he ordered the troops to stay in place until reinforcements reached them, at which time they should take Culp's Hill. Ewell was also concerned about the safety of his left flank.

Most of Ewell's subordinates were unhappy with this decision, wishing for a Stonewall Jackson, whom they felt would have attacked. A South Carolina lieutenant later wrote that: 'Our generals should have advanced immediately on that hill. It could have been taken then with comparatively little loss and would have deprived the enemy of that immense advantage of position which was afterward the cause of his success.' At any rate, the result was that there were no major Confederate attacks that day, although skirmishing along the lines went on well after dark.

While Ewell was considering what to do, Lee met Longstreet at Lee's headquarters on Seminary Ridge at about 5 o'clock. Longstreet, always a defensive fighter, saw an opportunity to turn the Union left, getting between him and Washington and forcing him to fight on good defensive ground of Confederate choosing. Lee, however, disagreed, determining to attack again next morning.

Ewell did not know that the Federal XII Corps was en route to Gettysburg, The first elements of that corps arrived at Two Taverns at about 3 p.m. and heard artillery fire in the distance, which would grow louder about thirty minutes later. Slocum, still under the impression that the battle would be along Pipe Creek, halted there, waiting for orders from Meade and failing to send a courier into Gettysburg to find out what was happening there. At about 1 o'clock he received word from XI Corps advising him of the fighting on the left wing of the Army of the Potomac against Hill's Corps at Gettysburg, with Ewell expected on the field. The message conveyed no sense of urgency, and Slocum decided to wait for his entire corps at Two Taverns, in accordance with Meade's original orders.

At 3.30, however, he learned from one of his staff members that heavy fighting was indeed going on at Gettysburg, and he began sending his corps to the aid of the rest of the army there. As they closed in on the town they could hear the sounds of the decisive Confederate attack on Seminary Ridge. Moving at the double quick in the hot July weather, men began falling out on the way, unable to keep up. Slocum himself helped rally fleeing Federals, having first turned over his corps command to senior divisional commander Brigadier General Alpheus Williams. At about seven he arrived on Cemetery Hill and assumed command from Hancock, who then took over the army's left wing. Slocum was unhappy at having to take over command of what he felt to be a disaster in the making. He wrote to Meade, 'Matters do not appear well ... I hope the work for the day is nearly over.'

In fact, by then it was, since Ewell did not resume the attack, and while field commanders drew up their lines as best they could, with one division of XII Corps based on Wolf Hill and the other on the Taneytown Road behind Cemetery Ridge, the I and XI Corps on Cemetery Hill, and Buford's cavalry near where the Emmitsburg Road crossed Seminary Ridge. At about 6 o'clock that evening lead elements of III Corps reached the southern part of the battlefield. These troops were assigned a position on the Union left. The rocky soil made it impossible for troops to dig any type of entrenchments so they formed loose lines, behind out-croppings, isolated boulders and stone walls.

There were still outbreaks of localised violence. At about six the 7th Indiana was sent to the top of Culp's Hill, where they began to build defences as best they could. A couple of Confederate scouts also reached the top of that hill, apparently just before the Indiana troops did, and they reported to Ewell that the position was clear of Federal troops. Ewell's subordinates urged the reluctant commander to take the position rapidly. He eventually ordered this to be done, but Confederate skirmishers ran into the 7th in position and reported the hill held by a superior force. Since the hill was no longer unoccupied, the Confederate brigade commander decided not to try to take it, and this put an end to Confederate attacks for the day.

That evening Lee visited Ewell and his divisional commanders and told them that he wanted to attack the Federals at first light. Ewell pointed out that the rocky ground would be hard to take, and suggested that the two Round Tops on the other side of the Federal line would be an easier proposition and result in a more conclusive victory. Lee then asked if he could withdraw his corps and march around Seminary Ridge to take the Round Tops. Ewell thought it would be bad for his men's morale if they left such good defensive ground for which they had fought so hard, and he might well have to leave his wounded behind. Lee left the meeting, still undecided as to whether his attack the next morning should be on the left or right, although he was moved by Ewell and his generals' arguments.

On the other side of the field Meade arrived at II Corps, just south of the Round Top, at about 11 o'clock and met the corps' temporary commander, Brigadier General John Gibbon. He then took the Taneytown Road heading for Cemetery Hill where he arrived at about midnight. He met his generals at the gatehouse where they were sitting on the floor in a room lit by a single candle. All the subordinates agreed that this was the place to fight this battle, and Meade indicated that he was glad of that because it was too late to pull back and fight elsewhere. After the meeting, the various generals headed off to their commands, while Meade walked over to East Cemetery Hill to check the position personally. Then he rode, accompanied by Generals Howard and Hunt, along Cemetery Hill to examine the entire line. He did not return until daybreak.

At Confederate headquarters, Lee eventually decided that Ewell had moved too far forward and should fall back next day to be more in line with Hill's men, and dictated a note to this effect. When Ewell received the note he went to Lee's headquarters in the Lutheran Seminary to restate his argument about not abandoning the ground he'd so far taken. Next morning, he said, he'd attack again and take Culp's Hill if it had not already been occupied. Lee approved, and Ewell returned to his headquarters and later received word to attack when he heard the guns of Longstreet's attack on the Union right next morning. By now it was almost daybreak and the first day of battle was over.

2 JULY

Lee's battle on 2 July would actually be two different battles: Ewell's attack on the left against Culp's and Cemetery Hills, and Longstreet's attack on the right on Little Round Top and Cemetery Ridge. Neither of these fights affected the other, and they were really separate actions.

On the left during the night Union troops had taken advantage of the darkness to build as many breastworks as possible along the crest of Culp's Hill, anchored on the left at Spangler's Spring. More Federals were to the left of them in McAllister's Woods, just above Rock Creek. Meade was interested in this area

Lee made his headquarters in this stone building, now a private museum and gift shop.

because he was considering using XII Corps and V Corps, which had come up earlier, to attack the Confederates east of Gettysburg. At about 9.30 he asked Slocum to reconnoitre the ground there. Half an hour later he told Slocum he would order his attack as soon as VI Corps arrived on the field. Slocum, however, accompanied by Meade's chief engineer, Warren, discovered that the ground they could take would not be worth the losses. Moreover, as it turned out, VI Corps was not to arrive until late in the afternoon.

At about 7 a.m. elements of V Corps arrived from the east beyond Wolf Hill. At first they stayed there, as part of Meade's attack plan, but when he abandoned that plan at about 10 o'clock he had V Corps sent to the right of XII Corps. This allowed II Corps to shift towards Cemetery Ridge, south through Ziegler's Grove toward the George Weikert House. III Corps was then given a line from the left of II Corps to the Round Tops, and got into position in mid morning.

Lee also looked that morning at the ground east of Gettysburg as a potential area for attack. He too sent an engineer, Major Charles Venable, from his staff to confer with the general on the ground there, and Venable and Ewell rode along the front, looking for potential areas of attack. Before the two had finished this tour, Lee himself, at about nine, rode over to Ewell's headquarters. Ewell returned from his ride before Lee left, and the two walked over the ground. Both agreed to postpone his attack until Longstreet on the right attacked, and then Ewell's assault would be a diversionary action, although Lee suggested that if success appeared possible, Ewell should go ahead on a full-scale attack. Because of the length of time it would take for Longstreet to get into position, the attack was set for about four that afternoon.

Unlike the previous day which had started with a shower, this daybreak was bright, and the sun beat down unmercifully on the troops. At places skirmishers exchanged shots. Most of Ewell's men were forced to sit in this direct sunlight, a small percentage being able to find odd spots of shade, while the Federals took advantage of the time to reinforce the works they had steadily improved in the Culp's Hill area. Many Confederate units found themselves in places where it was unsafe to stand up, and had to spend the hours sitting or lying in the sun. Other Confederates in the town sniped at the enemy from upper floor windows. Cannoneers fired on enemy batteries. On both sides of the front line company commanders sent off individuals with loads of canteens to get water, while other soldiers tried nearby farmhouses for food.

The more that III Corps' commander, Dan Sickles, examined his assigned position the more unhappy he became. Not far ahead of his line he saw higher ground near the intersection of the Wheatfield and Emmitsburg Roads, a ground now known as the Peach Orchard, which he liked much better. His right on the Emmitsburg Road would be just south of the Codori Farm, advanced and in front of the II Corps position, and his left would angle back to Devil's Den, opposite Little Round Top. He sent word back that he'd like Meade to come over and

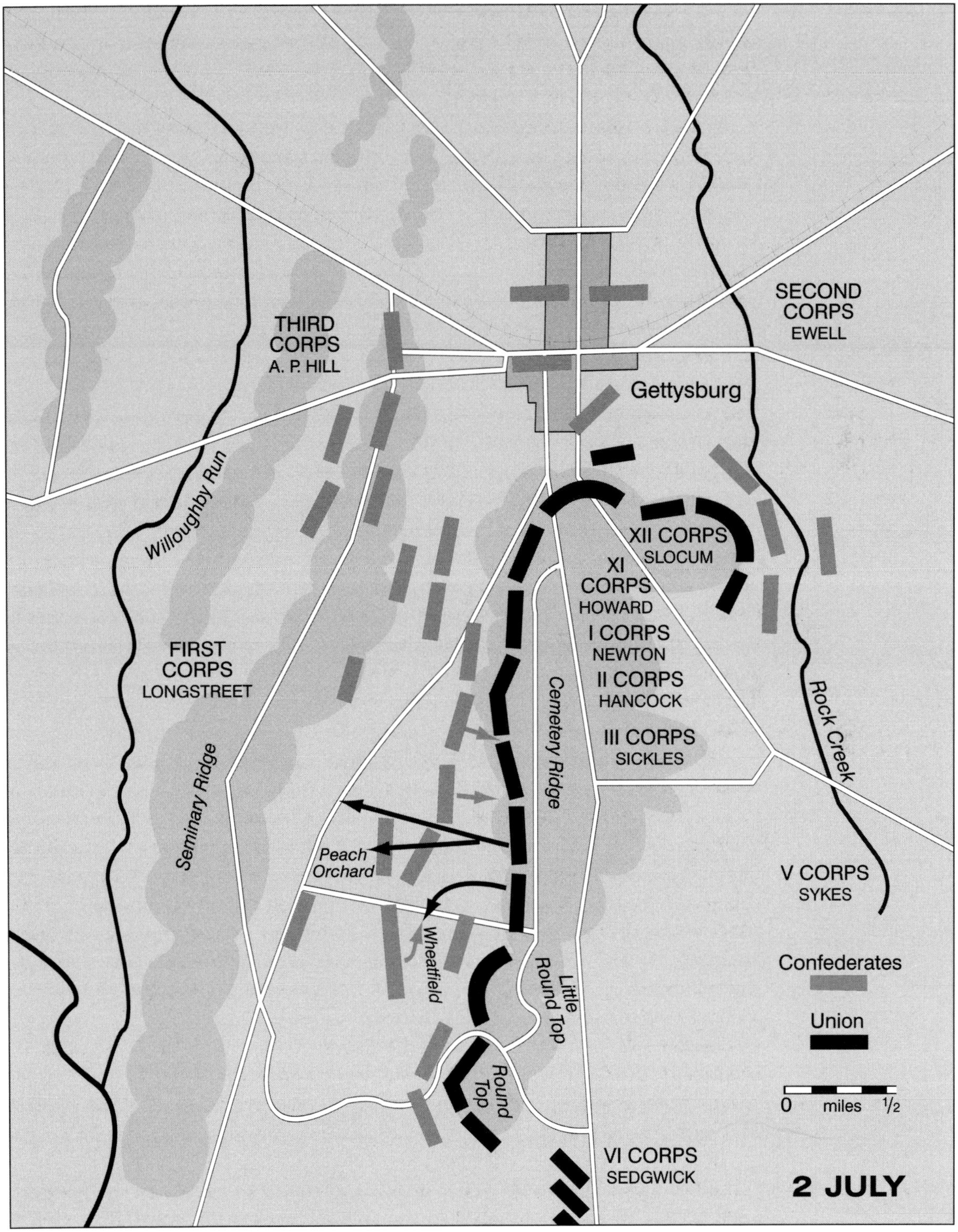
SECOND
CORPS
EWELL
THIRD
CORPS
A. P. HILL
Gettysburg
Willoughby Run
XII CORPS
SLOCUM
XI
CORPS
HOWARD
I CORPS
NEWTON
II CORPS
HANCOCK
III CORPS
SICKLES
FIRST
CORPS
LONGSTREET
Cemetery Ridge
Rock Creek
Seminary Ridge
Peach
Orchard
V CORPS
SYKES
Wheatfield
Little
Round Top
Confederates
Union
Round
Top
0 miles 1/2
VI CORPS
SEDGWICK
2 JULY

approve this move, but Meade was unavailable and sent his artillery commander, Henry Hunt, instead. Hunt saw both problems and possibilities in the position, and, while not authorising Sickles to move, rode back to Meade's headquarters to explain the situation.

In the meantime, Berdan's Sharpshooters, a unique green-clad unit armed with breech-loading Sharps rifles, reconnoitred towards Pitzer's Woods, where they found Confederates in much stronger numbers than expected and barely escaped without major losses. While this was going on Sickles sent another messenger to Meade's headquarters asking about his proposed move. Receiving no specific word, he decided to advance to the proposed position. He ordered his men forward, and by about 1 p.m. they had moved across the field to the position that Sickles believed was much better.

Meade, wondering what Sickles was up to and having been told by his chief engineer at about 3 p.m. that III Corps was not in its ordered position, sent word that the corps commander should report to headquarters. Sickles felt that to remain with his men was more important than going to a meeting, and declined. A second invitation was sent and declined, and Meade sent a peremptory order to meet. Sickles then rode over and Meade met him still mounted, and ordered III Corps to return to its original location.

Sickles and his staff headed back to his command, Meade and some staff officers following. They caught up with Sickles by the Wheatfield Road, from where Meade could see the new III Corps position. After a brief discussion in which Meade offered doubts about Sickles' ability to hold his new position, he grudgingly agreed to let the troops remain where they were, and rode back to his headquarters, while Sickles advanced the rest of his troops to their new position. It was now close to 4 p.m.

The last of Meade's corps, VI Corps, arrived on the field in mid afternoon after a hard-pushed route march of some thirty miles. With this all the Federal infantry, save for odd lots such as wagon train guards and the like, were on the field. They went into a camp in the Rock Creek area, replacing V Corps which then moved to the Union left.

On the Confederate right Longstreet was also on the move. He had met Lee early that morning, together with Hill who spent only a short time at Lee's headquarters. Earlier Lee had sent scouts, engineers among them, to reconnoitre the Federal left, and they were present when Longstreet arrived. After some discussion about unit placement and the wisdom of an attack, which Longstreet opposed, Lee ordered the attack on the Federal left at about 11 a.m. Longstreet would attack *en echelon*, starting with an assault through Devil's Den to take the Round Tops. If this attack was succeeding, Anderson's Division of Hill's Corps was to move up and strike the Federal centre on Cemetery Ridge by brigades. Ewell's men would divert Meade's attention on his right.

Anderson got his division into position in the early afternoon, then waited until Longstreet began his attack. Longstreet was to be slow in starting to get into position, however, because he was waiting for Law's Brigade, which was on its way from New Guilford where it served as a rear guard, to arrive. Some time after noon Law's Brigade arrived, and the entire column started off.

The column went down Herr Ridge, past the Black Horse Tavern, and left, crossing the Fairfield Road. Suddenly, however, the divisional commander at the head of the column, Layfayette McLaws, signalled a halt. He could see Union signal men on top of Little Round Top who obviously had a clear view of the advancing Confederates, and if they saw such numbers moving forward, could easily call up reinforcements. While the men waited, he sent men out to look for a better route, and rode back towards the rear of the column. He met Longstreet, who was concerned about the halt, and gave him the bad news.

Longstreet agreed that exposure at this point would be dangerous, and ordered the column to take the alternate route that McLaws proposed. In the hot sun, the men turned round and went back to Herr's Ridge the way they had come. From there they marched down a country road to Willoughby Run. With the hot, dry weather, the creekbed was dry, and the Confederates used this as a route to Pitzer's Schoolhouse on the other side of Pitzer's Woods. The going was slow over rough terrain and fences. At times the way was so narrow that the usual 4-man column had to be reduced to a 2-man column which made it even longer. At the schoolhouse they turned left, heading up the west slope of Seminary Ridge. As the Confederates emerged from the tree line on Seminary

Devil's Den from the east. The 4th Maine held a position on the right of the photograph until the Confederates cleared the entire position in the late afternoon of 2 July and held it until the battle's end, sniping at Union troops on Little Round top from their rocky position. Actually, only one cave in the mass of works was originally known as Devil's Den, but the name now embraces the entire area.

Ridge, Federal artillery opened fire. The Confederates deployed into line of battle, sending skirmishers to the front. Commanders ordered their artillery up. Hood's Division, the other division in this attack, followed McLaws', and went into line of battle, officers and men alike hot, thirsty and tired. It was now about 4 o'clock in the afternoon.

While they were waiting John Bell Hood, one of Longstreet's divisional commanders, argued against a frontal attack over the rocky ground in front of his division. He urged that they pass around Big Round Top, then strike the enemy's rear, with all its wagons free for the taking. Longstreet, however, refused, saying that Lee had specifically ordered this attack to take place, and he was to follow orders.

With that, Hood returned to his division, taking a place in front of his old command, the Texas Brigade. After making a brief speech, at about 4.30 he ordered fixed bayonets and forward march straight ahead. Alabama troops on the right flank would make for the Round Top, the remainder to head for the Devil's Den and Rose's Woods, held by Birney's division. As the troops marched forward, Hood went to a point just west of the Bushman barn. There, while watching his men advance, a shell exploded in the air above him. One piece of shrapnel smashed into his right arm, and Hood reeled from the blow. A staff member caught him, and he was lowered to the ground. Stretcher-bearers took him away. The division was now without its commander. A brigade commander, Evander Law, assumed command, but exercised little control in action.

As the attack pressed forward, gaps forced by the Emmitsburg Road and clumps of woods, opened in the line. No divisional commander was available to put things right, and the division became badly split, some of its units ending up with Law's Division to their left. Federal artillery opened up, but the Confederates pressed forward, driving back Federal skirmishers in Rose's Woods

In front of Devil's Den, Hood's lead brigades attacked Federals positioned between the Plum Run, across the west slope of Little Round Top, and edged by Rose's Woods. Two Texas Brigade regiments, 1st Texas and 3rd Arkansas, went into Rose's Woods, while the 4th and 5th Texas became mixed up with Alabama troops heading towards Devil's Den and the Little Round Top. Major General George Sykes, V Corps' commander, was on the scene and, worried about the weakness of the left flank, offered to send troops into the Wheatfield so that Birney could move more troops into Devil's Den. In fact, Meade had earlier advised him that a brigade might well be needed to reinforce Sickles. Before this could happen, Birney shifted several regiments from their right to defend the Devil's Den area, while the 4th Maine moved to a position between Rose's Woods and Devil's Den. Casualties were heavy: the 20th Indiana lost 146 out of 268 men on the field in less than half an hour.

The Confederates made progress into Devil's Den, but only slowly. On top of Little Round Top, Warren saw the danger in having so few men, only a signal party in fact, in this vital position, and sent word to Meade that troops were needed there. Not waiting for his reaction, he also sent word to Sickles, who refused, saying that he already had his hands full where he was. Warren's messenger then went to Sykes, who quickly ordered one of his brigade commanders to move on to the hill, but then decided to keep all his brigades and advance the entire corps to defend that area. On his way back, Warren's messenger ran into the lead brigade of V Corps, commanded by Strong Vincent, who, after a short conversation, decided to take his brigade to defend Little Round Top. Quickly the troops filed into position, the 20th Maine, led by a college professor, Joshua Chamberlain, taking the extreme left flank. They would be supported by Battery D, 5th US Artillery, whose men manhandled their guns to the top of the hill where, even if they could not depress the muzzles sufficiently, they knew they would put heart into the infantry by firing.

In Devil's Den, while Vincent's Brigade was moving up, the 124th New York counter-attacked the advancing Texans, driving them back down the slope. The regiment's major fell in the charge and the New Yorkers, under heavy fire, were halted. Making a stand, the regiment's lieutenant colonel was next wounded. Neither side, however, tried to advance, although heavy firing continued. Then Confederate commanders called for a renewed attack on Devil's Den and Union artillery in the area. They worked their way around the Federal right, and the 124th, together with the 86th New York and 20th Indiana, were ordered to fall back. While they were doing so, the 1st Texas reached a battery of three abandoned Union Parrott rifles.

Again Federals, this time from the 4th Maine and 99th Pennsylvania, counter-attacked on the ridge over Devil's Den, and again recaptured it. But they in turn were hit by the 20th Georgia which took the much fought-over ground. The two Federal regiments lost more than a third of their men.

The Wheatfield. Longstreet's men attacked from the left and rear, while Union counter-attacks came from the front and right.

More Federal troops, this group led by the 40th New York, formed into line and charged into the Plum Run Valley to plug the gap that had been opened by the recent Confederate advances. Men from the 2nd and 17th Georgia, positioned in the Slaughter Pen and the open area between that and Devil's Den, were forced back, but reformed by Devil's Den, where their new line held. Devil's Den was in Confederate hands.

Now men of the 4th and 5th Texas turned towards Little Round Top, running into skirmishers from the right flank of Vincent's Brigade. On his right, the 47th and 15th Alabama Regiments also advanced (they were suffering from thirst because, obliged to march off in a hurry, they had had to leave their canteen-carriers behind). On the way they ran into skirmishers from the 2nd US Sharpshooters, who fell back to Big Round Top. The Confederate commander, concerned about his right flank, detoured away from Little Round Top to follow them up the taller hill. The Federal skirmishers fell back in front of them, and the exhausted Alabamians halted on the summit of Big Round Top, from where they must have seen quite a scene spread before them. A Confederate staff officer found them there and ordered them to press on and take Little Round Top. Over the protests of the Alabama commander, the orders stood, and the weary men moved down the slope towards where the 20th Maine were standing on the Union left flank.

With little if any coordination with the regiments attacking Vincent's right, the two Alabama regiments attacked Chamberlain's position. The Maine boys held. The Confederates fell back, a regimental adjutant taking a party to try to turn the 20th's left flank. Chamberlain lengthened his line and pulled his left back into an 'L' shape. While the Texas troops, with the 4th Alabama, were held by Vincent's right and front, the attack on the 20th was renewed. Again the 20th held, but ammunition was getting low. Another attack was held off. But the Alabama troops, now under fire from the US Sharpshooters who had advanced on their right, had had enough, and began to fall back. At the same time Chamberlain, believing his men could not take another attack, ordered fixed bayonets for a charge. One of his company commanders, wanting to clear his wounded from the front, ran forward to get them, while men, waiting for the order to charge saw him go and assumed the order had been given. They started down the hill towards the Confederates, and Chamberlain, seeing them, quickly gave the order and the rest of the regiment followed. The Confederates, already beginning to pull out, were quickly overrun. As darkness began to fall, the left flank was secured.

But that was not the end of the fighting there. Sykes' Third Brigade, earmarked to support Sickles if needed, was instead ordered to support fighting on the left, and advanced into the Tostle's Farm area. From there it rushed to support Vincent's Brigade, forming on its left flank. With that the position was secure. Hood's men had taken Devil's Den, from where they sniped at Federals on Little Round Top, but had not been able to turn the Federal left.

At about the time when Hood was wounded, a little before five, Confederate Brigadier General George T. Anderson advanced north-east of the Timbers buildings and moved into Rose's Woods, supporting Hood's brigade on his right. His Confederates pushed Federals back, advancing to the cover of the Plum Run bank. There, under heavy Federal fire, the attack, made by exhausted, overheated men, stalled. Anderson ordered the brigade to fall back and reform, and was wounded in the right thigh while checking on his right flank. The slight lull in the fighting here ended when, at about 6 p.m., Kershaw's Brigade moved out of Biesicker's Woods, crossed the Emmitsburg Road, and moved into and through Rose's Woods. Its well-disciplined lines were broken up by Federal artillery in the Peach Orchard and infantry that had moved into Rose's Woods from their old position in Trostle's Woods.

Still the Confederates pressed on, charging again and again and finally driving the Federals to a point in Trostle's Woods near the Wheatfield Road. Federal artillery, with the 3rd Maine Infantry, in the Peach Orchard had to fall back as Kershaw's South Carolinians reached the Wheatfield Road. With this Sickles' left flank was falling apart. Word went to Hancock to send troops to the threatened position, between III and V Corps. Hancock quickly sent a division which soon passed the Trostle house and entered Trostle's Woods between the Trostle house and the Wheatfield Road. They then deployed into line of battle facing the Wheatfield and counter-attacked across the road, smashing into the Georgia troops in Rose's Woods, and turning Kershaw's flank. Kershaw's 7th South Carolina refused its right flank to defend its position on Stony Hill. A Federal brigadier general, Samuel Zook, was mortally wounded in the attack on Kershaw's troops.

This point was held by the 41st Pennsylvania and faces the Peach Orchard through which Barksdale's and Wofford's brigades struck III Corps in the afternoon of 2 July.

The Confederates here were also reinforced by a Georgia brigade led by Paul Semmes, who was mortally wounded here, which entered Rose's Woods and came to Kershaw's aid. But the 7th were finally forced to fall back, together with some of Semmes' men. The Wheatfield was again in Federal hands, leaving Devil's Den as the only part of the Union line well in Confederate hands after a fierce afternoon of battle. However the Confederates did not give up easily. They rallied and poured heavy fire into the new Union position, from right and left. The Federals finally had to fall back, moving slowly and bringing off their wounded.

Two brigades of US Army regulars from V Corps now crossed Plum Run towards Rose's Woods where they would be in a position to rake the right of the Confederate line assaulting the Wheatfield. Quickly they came under fire not only from the troops to their front, but from those in Devil's Den on their left, and they fell back to a position where their left was anchored by Little Round Top and their right by another brigade.

At about 6.15 two more brigades from McLaws' Division, supported by a great deal of artillery, moved out of Pitzer's Woods, across the Emmitsburg Road, towards the Peach Orchard. Federal artillery was especially effective against this attack, despite equally heavy Confederate counter-battery fire. Finally, however, the Federal guns had to limber up and pull out as Confederate infantry advanced. The Federal line, starting in the Peach Orchard along the Emmitsburg Road, crumbled from the left, and the men fled back towards Cemetery Ridge, leaving behind large numbers of dead and wounded. The Confederate artillery

The scene from the position of the 4th Texas Infantry, looking east towards Little Round Top. On 2 July the Texans would attack up this rocky slope towards the left, a position held by the 16th Michigan Infantry.

commander advanced a number of his guns to a point on the Emmitsburg Road where they could fire on Cemetery Ridge.

Now Sickles himself, riding towards the Trostle barn, was struck in the leg by a spent round shot and was carried from the field, David Birney assuming corps command. His first order was to pull the Corps left back to a point between his right, still advanced, and the Round Tops. Unfortunately by now the Federal units were too disorganised to do this easily, and the troops fled to Cemetery Ridge where, the Confederates being equally disorganised and unable to pursue, they were rallied and formed a new battle line. Anderson's Division, of A. P. Hill's Corps, now attacked from Spangler's Woods across the Emmitsburg Road, slowly driving the troops of III Corps' right flank, still firing, half a mile back to Cemetery Ridge.

The Pennsylvania Reserves (two brigades) counter-attacked against the mixed brigades of Kershaw, Semmes, and Anderson, then along the Plum Run, meeting stiff resistance and only slight local successes. The Confederates had formed their line in Devil's Den, along the Plum Run, and on the eastern side of Trostle's Woods. As darkness fell (the sun set at about 7.30) to end the fighting, III Corps finally found itself back where it had started before Sickles disobeyed Meade's orders and moved forward. Meade ordered Hancock to assume command of III Corps as well as his own.

On the right of III Corps, several II Corps regiments moved forward to the Codori house on the Emmitsburg Road, from where they could fire on the advancing Confederates to their left. Seeing this, Anderson advanced Ambrose Wright's and Carnot Posey's Brigades towards the Emmitsburg Road. Posey's Brigade, on the left, moved towards the Bliss house which was occupied by Federal troops. After a short firefight, in which the Federals ran short of ammunition, the Federals fell back to the Emmitsburg Road. At the same time, Wright's men dashed across the Emmitsburg Road and drove the Federals out of the Codori farmyard area; most of Posey's men remained in the Bliss farm area and did not contribute to this attack.

Wright's men reached a stone wall in front of a clump of trees being held by Webb's Philadelphia Brigade, and pushed the Federals back. But, badly outnumbered, they had to halt there and hope for support. This was coming because two Confederate brigades were advancing on the left of the position. The Federal line was coming apart. Quickly Hancock ordered the 1st Minnesota Regiment, heavily outnumbered, to counter-attack the advancing Confederates, buying time at the cost of lives. They moved out immediately, shaking the disorganised Confederates with a volley and then moving into the cover of Plum Run's bed. Confederate counter-attacks around the right poured heavy fire into the regiment. Still, Wilcox saw no supports coming, and ordered his men to pull back. As pressure on the 1st diminished, the regiment, now numbering only 47 officers and men, dashed back to Cemetery Ridge. Of all who had begun the fight, 82 per cent were now casualties.

On the right, the Confederates who had taken the stone wall also realised that they were not going to be supported, and returned to Spangler's Woods as Federal units swarmed around them to drive them back.

Further support for Longstreet's attack on the right and Hill's on the centre was to be supplied by Ewell's men on the left, who were to attack at 4 o'clock in the afternoon, coinciding with Longstreet.

Meade saw that his right flank on Culp's Hill was not being pressed hard, although there had been artillery duels and skirmishing all day. Therefore, because his left was being hit hard by Longstreet he ordered Slocum to send elements of XII Corps to move from the right to the left. Slocum thought such a move was unsafe, as it badly weakened the position on the right, but he did send all but one brigade to the aid of III Corps. As darkness fell, however, fighting on the left died down, while Johnson's Division of Ewell's Corps, some 4,000 officers and men in three brigades, finally struck the Federals on Culp's Hill at about 7 o'clock.

Defending the area were all that was left of XII Corps: a brigade of five New York regiments, some 1,350 strong, led by Brigadier General George S. Greene, a West Point-trained officer. Greene's troops had taken advantage of the time to construct breastworks across an already rough terrain. When the remainder of XII Corps pulled out, Greene extended his front to the right so as to occupy as much as possible of the works other units had already constructed.

When the Confederates hit, Greene asked for help and the 6th Wisconsin, 14th Brooklyn, 82nd Illinois, 61st Ohio, and 45th, 147th and 157th New York, were sent. Not all got there easily, some troops becoming confused in the dark woods, although when in the clear they could see their way by moonlight. The rest were of material help in holding the post. Federal fire and terrain that included woods, boulders and the Rock Creek greatly broke up Confederate attacking units. In confusion, the 1st North Carolina ended up firing into the 1st Maryland Battalion, CSA, for a time before the mistake was discovered. On the Confederate left, the 23rd Virginia reached works abandoned by XII Corps units, and swung to their right to enfilade Greene's flank.

The Virginians joined the Marylanders to attack these works, and quickly cleared them. It was now 8 o'clock, and the Federals refused their right flank to face this new threat. Hancock also sent two regiments from Webb's Brigade to help out, although one of them, the 106th Pennsylvania, ended up marching back and forth to no purpose. The other, the 71st Pennsylvania, reached the threatened right flank just in time to run into the Confederate attack. After losing but three officers and eleven enlisted men, the 71st retreated, leaving the Confederates in possession of the lower part of Culp's Hill, the 137th also having been forced to retreat.

Several Union regiments that had come up slowly through the dark woods, however, arrived in time to hold the line, halting the Confederate attack. As firing died down, the Confederates heard the sound of wagons that suggested a

Federal retreat. This was incorrect; in fact, the position had been further reinforced by two brigades. In the darkness, they moved to take over the Federal right flank. Both sides rested very close to each other, in places only a narrow tree line separating them. Both sides sent out small parties to reconnoitre the other's positions and individual firefights continued for hours.

The other major part of Ewell's diversionary effort was an attack on XI Corps' position on Cemetery Ridge, in front of the Baltimore Pike and just west of Culp's Hill, in which two brigades that had moved out from their positions just east of Gettysburg at about 7.30 took part. The Federal units there had taken quite a beating the day before and were considerably under strength. Still, their position was strong, many of the men being able to take advantage of a stone wall that ran along the road that they were defending. Federal artillery opened fire as soon as the advancing Confederates were seen, although darkness and low ground prevented their fire from being very effective at first.

The Confederates struck at a point where the Federals had refused their left and the Ohio troops there fell back up the hill towards their artillery. Other Federals held their positions, and hand-to-hand fighting was not uncommon. At this point the Confederate commander on the right, Colonel E. I. Avery, fell from his horse mortally wounded. In the darkness, nobody saw him fall, and the Confederates there were without a commander for the rest of the attack.

Federal artillery switched to canister as more and more Federal infantrymen began to fall back after fierce hand-to-hand fighting. But help was on the way. Howard pulled units from his right and sent them to the threatened position. He also sent word for help from Hancock who replied by sending the First Brigade, First Division, to his aid, two regiments, the 71st and 106th Pennsylvania, as noted above, going to Culp's Hill, and the rest going to the Cemetery Ridge fight. Other regiments, the 4th Ohio, 7th West Virginia, and 14th Indiana, also arrived to help out.

Confederate infantry actually penetrated the Federal gun line, but the attack had reached its apex. Federals swarmed over the position and drove back the disorganised Confederates. Not only did they save the guns, but they ended up capturing a number of Confederates of all ranks.

Confederate divisional commander Jubal Early, watching the attack from the town, had prepared John B. Gordon's brigade to reinforce the attack. However, as he saw it fall apart, he stopped Gordon from advancing, ordering him to hold his position as a point on which to rally the retreating troops from his other two brigades. The other support was to come from Robert Rodes' Division of Longstreet's Corps, which had been ordered to help Ewell's attack on the left. When he saw movement on his left, he began to move his troops forward, but when they deployed, in the moonlight, they could see the strength of the Union position. Moreover, Rodes learned that Ewell's attack had failed before he could get into the fight, and therefore he withdrew his men to Long Lane, where they dug in.

3 JULY

Finally the fighting drew to a close and first sergeants added up their losses for the day. It had been an expensive one, with some 16,500 dead, wounded or missing. The Confederates had lost more men as prisoners, while more Federals had been killed.

On the Confederate side Lee was satisfied with the day's activity. He felt that while not everything he'd wanted had come about, there were 'partial successes'; the lower end of Culp's Hill and higher ground in the Peach Orchard areas were in Southern hands. Even so, he was disappointed with what he felt was a 'proper concert of action' between his two flank attacks and various corps commanders. In fact, Lee had made no particular effort to be sure that such attacks were coordinated, having spent most of the afternoon watching the action from a post with A. P. Hill and Henry Heth near the Lutheran Seminary, notably sending only one message during the day. His staff not make sure plans were followed. Moreover, he must have been aware from personal observation that Hill exercised no command over his corps on the field, some of his men being pulled into Longstreet's attack, and others failing to support Ewell's. Nor was Ewell especially driving in his attacks. On the other hand, Longstreet and his staff had been personally involved in overseeing his complicated attacks over difficult terrain.

Nevertheless, Lee was pleased enough with his men's work that he planned essentially the same attacks for 3 July. Longstreet, using Pickett's Division, which had recently reached the field, would attack next morning, while Ewell would again hit the Union right at the same time. Ewell understood this to mean a daybreak attack, but Longstreet and Lee had not reached an understanding of exactly how and when this attack would be mounted because the two generals had failed to meet that evening, In fact it would be well into 3 July before the plan was formalised. Lee did not call his subordinates to his headquarters to discuss the plan, merely sending a general order to Longstreet calling for an attack the following morning, time not specified. Longstreet, who felt he was free to make this attack as would best suit himself, spent some time sending out scouts who found a way around the Federal left flank. He sent orders for his units to move in that direction in the morning. No specific orders were sent to Pickett's Division to prepare for an early morning attack.

At about 9 p.m. on the 2nd Meade had met his corps commanders and chief of staff, as well as his chief engineer, in his headquarters at the Leister house, just behind Cemetery Ridge. Warren, exhausted from the day's activities, did not participate in the round-table discussion, but fell asleep in a corner. The small group discussed the action of the day, the condition of the army, and logistical concerns; the army had outrun its supplies on the way to Gettysburg. All agreed that the army should stay where it was in a defensive position, although some adjustment on the left might be needed. If Lee failed to attack, they should consider taking the offensive. Meade then told Slocum that he was free to attack the Confederates in positions they'd taken that day. As the meeting broke up, he mentioned to John Gibbon, who had command of II Corps, that were Lee to attack next morning he suspected it would be on his front, the middle of the Union line. A surprised Gibbon asked why. 'Because he has tried my left and failed, and has tried my right and failed; now, if he concludes to try it again, he will try the centre, right on your front.' Gibbon replied, 'Well, general, I hope he does, and if he does, we shall whip him.'

Meade, however, was also concerned about his left flank. He told Hancock that he would keep his V and VI Corps there, where they could be used to attack the Confederate right when their attack on his centre failed. He then sent word to the army's general-in-chief, Henry Halleck, in Washington that he planned to fight it out at Gettysburg.

Slocum left the meeting and returned to his headquarters, ordering the temporary corps commander, Alpheus Williams, to drive out the Confederates on Culp's Hill at daylight. Williams, considering the roughness of the terrain for an infantry assault, decided to depend on artillery superiority and began siting his guns. Then, at about 3.30 a.m. on 3 July, Williams lay down on a flat rock for a quick nap.

Across the lines, Ewell's men were also preparing for their spoiling attack planned for this morning. The commander there brought up reinforcements and worked well into the night getting units into position. His orders, too, were to attack at daybreak.

At 4.30, as the night sky was beginning to brighten, Federal artillery opened up, along with musketry from the front-line infantrymen. In fact, hidden behind stone walls and captured breastworks, as well as trees and boulders, most of the Confederate infantry avoided injury from this gunfire, although some on the lower hill made good targets and had to be pulled back immediately. Some short rounds, however, fell among Union infantry, causing 'friendly fire' casualties. This firing went on, with brief lulls for refilling limber chests, for some six hours.

Despite this barrage, the Confederates, as ordered, went on the attack, beating the Federals to the punch. Indeed, Williams' troops stayed inside their works and fought off the Confederate attacks. On the Confederate left, however, the 1st Maryland, Potomac Home Brigade, moved to the attack, past Spangler's Spring, into the position held by the 2nd Virginia. Under heavy fire and with ammunition in short supply, the Marylanders were beaten back to their original position on the other side of the Baltimore Pike.

The attacking Confederates were also under heavy fire and running out of ammunition. Volunteers went to the rear and brought back wooden crates of ammunition, running a gauntlet of fire in the process. Attacking infantrymen were not only under fire from Federals behind breastworks towards the crest of the hill, but also on their left as the 20th Connecticut advanced into the area through which the 1st Maryland, Potomac Home Brigade, retreated, above Spangler's Spring, and opened fire. They would fight there until about 10 o'clock, pushing close to the stone wall that the Confederates held. More Federals came forward to relieve their hard-pressed, exhausted comrades at the front, even regimental commanders picking up rifle muskets to join in. But the Federal line held off one attack after another.

After the attack started Ewell received word that Longstreet's attack would be delayed until 9 o'clock and realised that his troops were attacking alone. Still, in mid morning, Major General Edward Johnson, the man who had been in charge of taking Culp's Hill for the Confederates, decided to make a third and final attack. One brigade, commanded by Marylander Brigadier George H. Steuart, would attack from the Spangler's Spring area on the left, the renowned Stonewall Brigade on the right, and a North Carolina brigade led by Junius Daniel between them. The brigade commanders whose commands had been so badly blooded in the previous attacks were not happy about making this final effort.

The Confederates formed their lines and attacked again, the nature of ground separating them into virtually two separate attacks on the right and left. The Marylanders on the left came to within some 40 yards of the Federal lines before overwhelming fire forced them back. Daniels' Brigade and the Stonewall Brigade on the right did not seem to get as close as did the Marylanders before they too were forced back. The final assault lasted no more than an hour. Many Confederates, left behind in the retreats, raised makeshift white flags and were brought into Federal lines.

The Confederates now formed new lines in the Rock Creek and Spangler's Spring area. At about 10 o'clock Thomas Ruger, who commanded the First Division, XII Corps, positioned north of the Baltimore Pike at a point between Spangler's Spring and McAlliser Hill, received orders to clear the Confederates out of the lower Culp's Hill area. He gave this job to Colonel Silas Colgrove's brigade. Colgrove ordered two regiments, as many as would fit in the area, to charge across an open meadow, towards Steuart's Brigade in the Spangler's Spring area. They attacked, but the 2nd Massachusetts were forced to fall back to the left, and the 27th Indiana were also stopped, and fell back towards their original position. However, the 20th Connecticut finally managed to reach the stone wall and the works beyond. Reinforced by the bayonet-charging 123rd New York, the XII Corps men finally cleared the lower Culp's Hill.

Ewell's attacks had been in vain; they had come too early to help Longstreet, and they failed to roll up the Federal right despite suffering extremely heavy losses. Johnson pulled back his division and the attack was over. But small fire fights and skirmishing lasted well into the night on the Federal right.

While Ewell was preparing his attack, Longstreet, too, was up and about, considering the day's move. Before dawn the general sent his report on the previous day's action and received word that Lee wanted yesterday's attack to be continued.

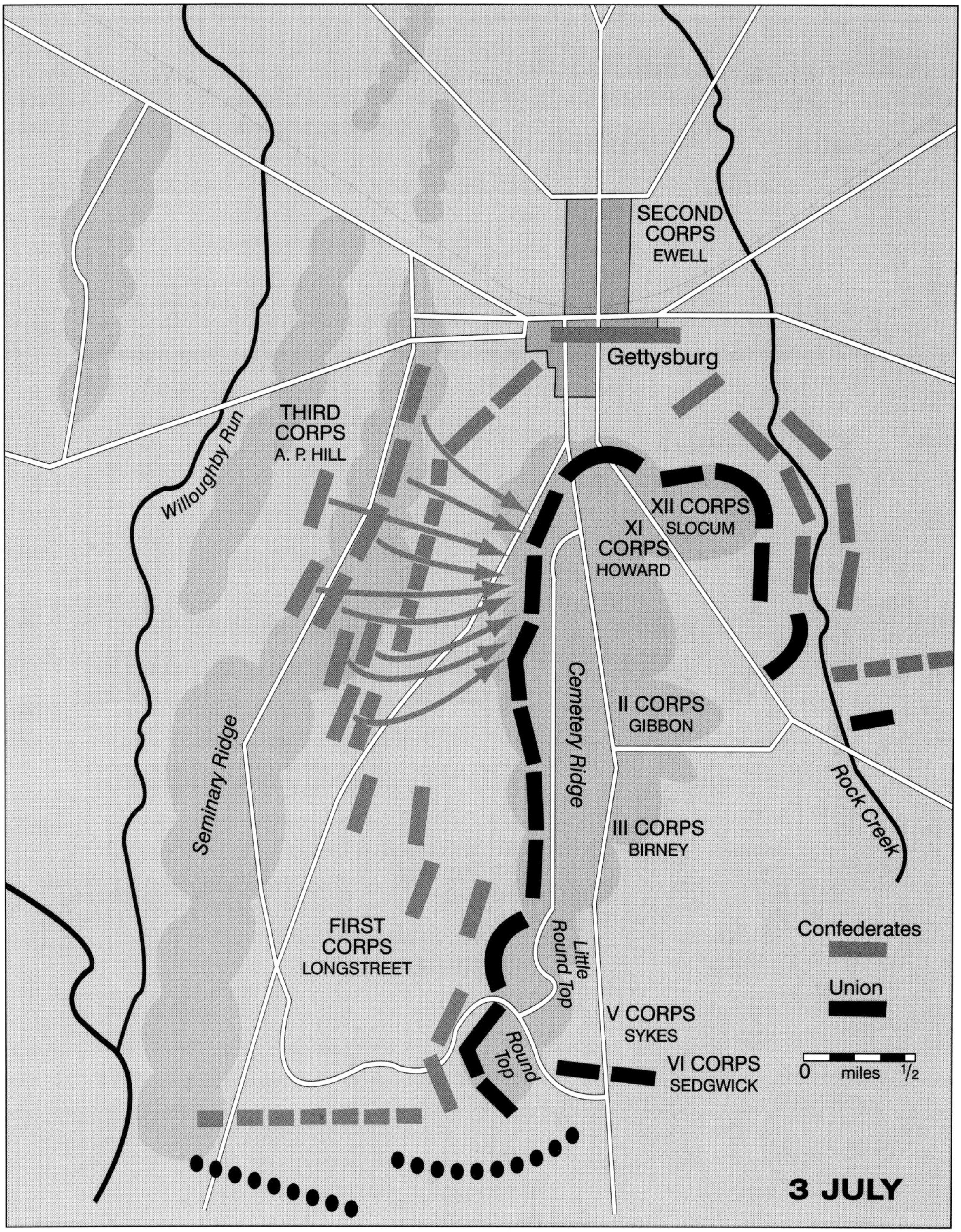
SECOND CORPS
EWELL
Gettysburg
THIRD CORPS
A. P. HILL
Willoughby Run
XII CORPS
SLOCUM
XI CORPS
HOWARD
II CORPS
GIBBON
Cemetery Ridge
Seminary Ridge
Rock Creek
III CORPS
BIRNEY
FIRST CORPS
LONGSTREET
Little Round Top
Round Top
V CORPS
SYKES
VI CORPS
SEDGWICK
Confederates
Union
0 miles 1/2
3 JULY

Longstreet felt that he had lost a large number of men for little or no real gain and didn't want to attack on the 3rd. Instead, he rode out to his right to see if he could slip his corps around the Round Tops and turn the Federal left. Encouraged by reports from his scouts, he began planning the move when Lee arrived at his headquarters, at about 4.30 a.m. The two men could hear the opening guns of Ewell's attack.

Lee was surprised by Longstreet's plan and cancelled it, ordering instead an assault by Longstreet's Corps on the southern end of Cemetery Ridge. In fact, he had thought this was understood and was disappointed that it was not already under way. Despite this delay, he still called for an assault to be made by Pickett's Virginia division, which had arrived only the day before and was still fresh, supported by the rest of the corps. Ewell's attack on the left, which had just got under way, would provide a diversion.

Longstreet, his opinion based on the previous day's action as well as his natural inclinations, strongly disagreed. He argued for his proposed slip around the Federal left instead. But Lee would have none of it. Longstreet later said that Lee pointed towards the Union centre and said, 'The enemy is there, and I am going to strike him.'

Longstreet, however, pointed out the danger of a frontal assault where the defenders on the Confederate flank would be withdrawn to participate. Federals there could bring any attacking forces under heavy fire, especially from artillery, and then would be free to counter-attack on the Confederate right. Lee saw the point and agreed that the divisions that were currently there should remain in place. As the two talked, they certainly understood that any chance of a coordinated attack was pretty well past unless Pickett's men could be rushed forward. They could not – the division was still not in place.

But Lee liked the basic idea of his original plan. He therefore changed his order of battle: Pickett's Division would continue as the spearhead, but troops from Hill's Corps would be brought in so that a total of some 15,000 men would make the attack. Longstreet thought that would not be enough, but Lee, having seen the result of what his men could do at Chancellorsville only a couple of months earlier, was sure of the result. Longstreet, less sanguine about the prospects, suggested that Hill should lead it, but Lee would not hear of it. With a heavy heart, Longstreet accepted his orders.

As part of the attack, Lee planned a heavy artillery concentration on the Clump of Trees and surrounding area to precede the infantry attack. Batteries from not only Longstreet's and Hill's Corps would be involved, but also many from Ewell's Corps which could bring enfilade fire to bear that would rake the entire Federal line. In all, on the signal of two shots from the Washington Artillery of New Orleans on Longstreet's right, some 159 cannon would open up on the Federals. The infantry would advance after enemy cannon had been driven from the ridge. Lee rode off to the left, towards Hill's men, to see about this artillery while Longstreet went off to get the attack organised.

He told Pickett to get his men into position, but that they should stay hidden as much as possible from Federal artillery ringing the ridge. Longstreet took his subordinate general personally to look over the objective from a point in the Confederate lines, as he and Lee had done earlier. Pickett was enthusiastic about his chances, which depressed Longstreet, because it seemed to him to indicate an unrealistic attitude. Then Longstreet told Brigadier General James J. Pettigrew, commanding Heth's Division of Hill's Corps in the absence of the wounded Heth, to attack in alignment with Pickett, on his left, although he did not take the North Carolinian to observe the objective as he had with Pickett. He told his artillery commander, E. P. Alexander, of the plan, which required a major artillery preparation to succeed at all, and ordered him to get all the guns possible in place. It would take some hours for Longstreet to complete his preparations, and he and Lee met again at various times until at least ten in the morning.

What Longstreet failed to do was to provide for any serious back-up if the attack managed to break through the Federal line. Lee's army was so thinly spread that a sufficiently large 'second wave' would be impossible to organise without severely weakening his line elsewhere. Instead, brigades on either flank were prepared to move forward, more as a shield to the main assault than as a second wave. In fact, it was Lee who let the brigade on the left, part of Hill's Corps, knowing that it would be used in the attack. and that its commander should report to Longstreet for details.

Longstreet communicated all his orders directly to Hill's subordinate commanders without going through Hill's headquarters, as would be the more normal practice. Hill himself, although large numbers of troops from his Corps would be involved, took no part in the planning, but was content with his orders to remain in line, and be ready to move forward should Longstreet meet with success.

Alexander, who learned the plan's details in a meeting with Lee and Longstreet at about 8 o'clock, was told that his guns must cripple the Federals in the objective area, and then as many as possible of them must be advanced to support the actual attack. Alexander had problems. He had only some 200 rounds for each of his corps' 75 guns; too few for a long bombardment since replacement ammunition would have to be hauled up from Staunton, in the Valley of Virginia. Ammunition would be needed after the attack, regardless of its success or failure. He estimated that the preliminary bombardment of some 30 well-aimed shots an hour, should last no longer than an hour. On this assumption, he had the corps' guns brought up and placed into position, the Washington Artillery, a high society pre-war New Orleans 4-battery battalion, on the right being given the job of firing the opening rounds as a signal for the rest.

To accompany the attack, he was also able to deploy about eight 12pdr howitzers, smoothbores with short ranges used mainly to break up infantry at fairly close range, which Hill's Corps artillery commander made available. He had these sent to a point near the Pitzer House, behind Spangler's Woods, with orders to be ready to move when sent for.

Long after the fight on Ewell's front was over, between 11 o'clock and noon, Alexander reported to Longstreet that the artillery was ready, but not all the infantry were yet in position, so he was told to wait. When they were ready, the signal guns would fire and the bombardment would begin. Alexander would have a special task. It would be he rather than Longstreet who would observe the effects of the fire and, when the time was right, order the actual attack. This did not bother Alexander, but a later message from Longstreet did: 'If the artillery fire does not have the effect to drive off the enemy, or greatly demoralize him, so as to make our efforts pretty certain, I would prefer that you should not advise Gen. Pickett to make the charge. I shall rely a great deal on your good judgment to determine the matter & shall expect you to let Gen. Pickett know when the moment offers.'

Alexander suddenly realised that Longstreet did not share the confidence of Lee, Pickett, and himself in the attack and was essentially passing the buck to his subordinate. He jotted a note to Longstreet saying that if an alternative to the attack could be considered, it should be done before the artillery opened fire. Once that happened, the small amount of ammunition available would be committed. Moreover, the thick fog of black powder explosions that would cover the front would make it difficult even to see the enemy's positions, let alone judge when it would be best for the infantry to move forward. At 12.15 Longstreet's

Alexander's gun line from where the bombardment of the Union centre on 3 July was made. Pickett's men hid in the woods behind the gun line and emerged to deploy into line just in front of the trees to begin their assault. The cannon are 12pdr Napoleons made in the Columbus, Georgia, Armory.

reply came: 'The intention is to advance the Infy. if the Arty. has the desired effect of driving the enemy's off, or having other effect such as to warrant us in making the attack.'

Alexander rode over to Brigadier General Ambrose Wright, whose brigade had attacked Cemetery Ridge in the same place yesterday as Pickett would today. Wright read the note and remarked that Longstreet had again passed the buck. Alexander agreed, and wondered how likely it would be for the attack to succeed. Wright said that the position could be taken, that his men had taken it the day before, but the problem would be staying there, 'for the whole infernal Yankee army is up there in a bunch'.

Alexander next went over to Pickett to see how he felt about the attack, and was reassured by his confidence. With that, he jotted a note to Longstreet saying, 'When our artillery fire is at its best I shall order Gen. Pickett to charge'. There was no backing out now. He called for the howitzers to come forward, so that any rocky woods between them and the front wouldn't delay them during the infantry's advance, and was dismayed to learn from his courier that the guns were not to be found. As it happened, army artillery chief Pendleton had come across them while touring his lines and, Alexander being occupied at the front, had simply ordered them to another position on the field. He neglected to tell Alexander about this change, as did the howitzer battery's commander.

Alexander's plan for close artillery support was thwarted, but he ordered Blunt's and Stribling's Batteries, in Dearing's Battalion of Longstreet's Corps, to join in for the first fifteen minutes of the opening barrage, and then move forward with the infantry, halting from point to point to give covering fire. The two battery commanders reconnoitred the field in front of them, over which they'd have to move, and found that the sunken Emmitsburg Road, lined by post-and-rail fences, would present a serious obstacle. The guns would have to pass it by column through a gate on the road, ride down the road in column, presenting an excellent target, to another gate a couple of hundred yards away, and then go through that gate and deploy back into battalion battle line. Nevertheless battalion commander James Dearing felt it was worth the try.

Pickett's men came up and into position as the generals and subordinates reconnoitred the front and made their plans. They had been up since 3 a.m., and had breakfast before marching to their new positions. On the way there was a brief halt for an ammunition issue. The general brought an estimated 5,830 infantrymen on to the field, deployed in three brigades. James Lawson Kemper's brigade was placed on the right in the Spangler Orchard, with Richard Brooke Garnett's brigade on its left. Lewis A. Armistead's brigade was behind them, just in front of Spangler's Woods. Kemper positioned his regiments, from the right: 24th, 11th, 1st, 7th, and 3rd Virginia. Garnett's 8th Virginia was next to the 3rd, and his other regiments, from the right were: 18th, 19th, 28th, and 56th Virginia. Armistead's regiments were, from the right: 9th, 53rd, 57th, and 38th Virginia.

Some of the infantrymen took advantage of the lull to stroll up to the front and look at their objective. Most came away with the feeling that success was unlikely, but that they would do their best if Lee called for the charge.

Pettigrew's Division, some 4,300 strong, was already on line, with Archer's brigade on the right, then Pettigrew's, Davis', and Brockenbrough's Brigades. Trimble's two brigades were placed behind Pettigrew's right. For support were Wilcox's and Lang's Brigades. Wilcox's Brigade was fronted on the orchard at D. Kingle's farm on the Emmitsburg Pike, with Lang to his left. The two brigades totalled some 1,700 men.

Across the field lay 5,750 Union infantrymen of II Corps. Gibbon's 2,150-strong division were holding Pickett's main objective. Webb's Philadelphia Brigade, in this division, was the unit posted at the Clump of Trees, with the 69th Pennsylvania, an Irish unit, actually holding that exact position, supported by Battery A, 4th US Artillery, and Battery B, 1st Rhode Island Light Artillery. The 71st Pennsylvania was to the right of Battery A, with 72nd Pennsylvania to the left, and 106th Pennsylvania beside them. Gibbon's Third Brigade was to the left of Webb's and the First Brigade was on the left of the division's line. Elements of I Corps on the left of II Corps would also become involved in this defence. In all, 3,785 Union soldiers were occupying the position that Longstreet's 5,830 troops would strive to capture.

At last, some minutes after 1 p.m., Confederate preparations were finished and Longstreet ordered the signal guns to open the artillery bombardment. Shells filled the air as the Federal infantry lowered their colours and struck shelter halves set up as protection against the beating sun. Federal artillery replied, and the noise was intense. The volumes of smoke were so heavy that at times visibility was down to twenty yards. One Federal artillery officer figured that each gun on the field was firing two to four rounds a minute.

In most places along the line, however, Federal infantry casualties were relatively few in number. Confederate artillery, firing towards Cemetery Ridge, was sending shells over their heads. Meade's headquarters in the Leister House took quite a beating, many horses being killed in the yards there. Meade was actually grazed by a small shot, while chief of staff Daniel Butterfield was hit in the side and taken away in an ambulance. Meade and his staff had to leave, going to a signal station on Powers Hill, near the Baltimore Pike. Union batteries on the crest were also badly hit.

Hunt reacted by calling up more artillery, while withdrawing some of the more damaged batteries. At the same time, he ordered some artillery silenced so as to save them for the infantry assault that was bound to follow. Hancock, riding along the line to inspire his men, saw some of these silent guns and, fearing the effect on his infantry, ordered them to resume firing. Most quit firing after Hancock left, and Hunt would not find out about Hancock's interference until the next day.

In fact, however, Federal artillery was doing more than simply boost the infantry's morale, it was also doing serious damage to the Confederate infantry lying in wait behind their gun line. Ambulance Corpsmen were busy carrying wounded from every brigade to their respective aid stations, and the horror of flying limbs as well as iron greatly affected Confederate morale. Between 300 and 800 men were lost in Pickett's Division alone, while the other units making the attack had proportionately fewer casualties.

After some 25 minutes of this barrage, Alexander saw no reduction in enemy counter-battery fire and began to worry about his ammunition supply. He jotted a note to Pickett: 'If you are able to advance at all, you must come at once, or we will not be able to support you as we ought. But the enemy's fire has not slackened materially, & there are still 18 guns firing from the cemetery.' Shortly afterwards Hunt's artillery substitution could be seen from the Confederate lines, Alexander believing that the Federal guns were simply being withdrawn. At 1.40 he wrote to Pickett, 'The 18 guns have been driven off. For God's sake come on quick, or we cannot support you. Ammunition nearly out.'

Pickett took this note over to Longstreet and asked if he should advance. Longstreet, overcome by dread at the thought of this attack, simply nodded his agreement, and Pickett rode off to move his men out while Longstreet rode off to join Alexander at the gun line. There he learned of the serious ammunition shortage, and told Alexander to stop Pickett until he could be resupplied. Alexander said this would take too long, and Longstreet simply allowed the game to be played out.

Just before 2 o'clock Pickett's lead brigades reached the gun line and marched past, towards the front. At that time the Confederate artillery fell silent, as did the Federals. For the first 100 yards Pickett's men marched forward as if on parade. His skirmish line was about 300 yards ahead of the division. 'It was a splendid sight to see,' later recalled one Connecticut soldier. On the left, Pettigrew, who had not been advised that Pickett was ready to move, advanced when Pickett's troops were already 300 yards from their starting positions. Only two of his brigades moved out on time. Brockenbrough's small Virginia brigade, lagged behind. His units, as a result, were more hurried and less firmly under control than were Pickett's.

At this point Federal artillery and infantry skirmishers opened fire, and the Confederates began to suffer casualties. The Confederate cannon assigned to support the attack also moved forward to the Emmitsburg Pike, where their cannoneers tore down fences to make firing lanes, while other guns moved up to the Sherfy barn. Short of ammunition, and badly battered by Federal cannon, the Confederate artillery in the event did little to support the attack.

On the far left, Brockenbrough's Brigade halted at the Bliss Farm to readjust lines. His men, however, were taking tremendous fire from infantry and artillery that had not been badly punished by the Confederate artillery. The 8th Ohio, in open order, counter-attacked, and fired a volley that essentially destroyed the Confederate brigade. Most of Brockenbrough's men broke and fled back to Seminary Ridge, although some remained in the Long Lane in skirmish order. Both Pettigrew and Pickett sent staff officers in a vain attempt to rally the Virginians.

As Pickett's men advanced up to the Emmitsburg Pike, on the left, Garnett's Brigade was ordered to shift left to guide on Pettigrew's right flank, with the other brigades following suit. Pickett himself stopped at the Sherfy peach orchard, from where he could observe the action. He sent word back to Longstreet from there asking for support. Longstreet sent word to Trimble to advance on the left, replacing Brockenbrough's broken brigade, and another courier was sent to see about moving up supports on the right.

Once the Confederates had begun to climb over the Emmitsburg Pike fences, the full line of Federal infantry opened fire. Torn by casualties, many Confederates simply halted in the sunken road and returned fire rather than cross the second fence and advance towards the stone wall. The colonel of the 7th Tennessee, part of Pettigrew's Division, reckoned that only about half his men actually crossed the first fence and fewer than fifty of them then crossed the second fence and went beyond it. The line of Confederates in the road was so strong that it looked to some observers like a formal battle line.

Davis' Brigade, now forming the left flank of the attack, made no effort to cross the road. There they were hit on their flank by the 8th Ohio and elements of the 125th New York. Under heavy fire, the Mississippi troops broke and fled to the rear. Now only some 1,000 men in Pettigrew's Division continued the attack, with

some 1,000 of Pickett's men on their right. Pickett's right was also in trouble, and he ordered a sharp left oblique to close up towards Pettigrew again. On their right, the Second Vermont Brigade advanced as did the 8th Ohio to fire into the Confederates from the flank as they passed through the buildings of the Codori farm. Pickett sent word back directly to Wilcox pleading for help, and Wilcox advanced his brigade, unfortunately not directly at the Vermonters, but rather south of them. This would effectively make his brigade, which had started too late anyway, unable to support Pickett's troops effectively.

Pickett's and Pettigrew's survivors were now 200 yards away from their objective, and those 200 yards were open, deadly ground, well covered by Federal infantry fire. Formal battle lines dissolved into mobs of armed men desperately advancing. Both Kemper and Garnett, then only a few yards from the wall, fell, and their brigades dissolved, men fleeing back towards the Emmitsburg Pike. Armistead's men kept coming, one private stopping at the wall to take out a watch and remark, 'We have been just nineteen minutes coming.'

On the left, some of Pettigrew's men made it to within 20 yards of the stone wall, which angled back on their front and was on higher ground, before his attack came to an end. Regimental colours lay among the wounded and dead as the Confederates dashed back again through a field of fire to the Emmitsburg Pike and beyond. Trimble himself was badly wounded once he reached the Emmitsburg Pike. Inside the stone wall on Pickett's front, some 100 Confederates, including Armistead, crossed the wall and found themselves among the abandoned Federal cannon there. But men of the 69th Pennsylvania stood strong at the right of Pickett's survivors, while more Federals poured in from all sides. There were no supports; the Confederate effort was finished. Armistead, having placed one hand on a gun barrel, fell, mortally wounded.

Codori Farm on the right; Clump of Trees on the left centre – Pickett's objectives.

As the battered Confederates fell back individually and in small groups, Lee rode down to meet them, admitting to all he met that the defeat was all his fault. Longstreet also met them, and attempted to set up a line for the counter-attack he firmly expected. In fact, the Union line was happy chaos as Meade rode along the line, happy enough just to have successfully defended it. After an hour, when it was almost 5 o'clock that afternoon, Longstreet realised that there would be no counter-attack, and sent orders for McLaws' and Hood's Divisions to fall back to the positions they had held on 2 July before attacking the Federal left.

These infantry fights were not the only action on 3 July, however. In the early morning Union cavalry commander Pleasonton had received orders from Meade to secure the position on the right of the XII Corps, along the Baltimore Pike, and the left flank around the Round Tops. Pleasonton ordered Judson Kilpatrick, a recent West Point graduate suddenly made a brigadier general, to take his division to the Round Tops and attack any enemy found there, while Gregg's division would hold the right.

Kilpatrick's men were encamped at Two Taverns and Pleasonton's orders reached him there at eight in the morning. Before he could begin to comply, he received orders detaching Custer's brigade to be posted at the intersection of the Hanover and Low Dutch Roads. Custer's men moved out, reaching their objective shortly after 9 o'clock. Once there they spotted Confederate cavalry to their front. These were Stuart's men, the wayward general having arrived at Lee's headquarters the previous day shortly after noon, with his men following. After a sharp and uncharacteristic rebuke by Lee, Stuart was ordered to post his men beyond Ewell's left flank. The exhausted cavalrymen were unable to start for this location until the morning hours of 3 July, with Stuart in the vanguard.

Stuart dismounted some of his men when they reached a point west of Cress Ridge, and advanced them on foot towards the Rummel farm. At the same time, he brought up a section of artillery to reconnoitre the Hanover and Low Dutch Road intersection 'with fire'. This stirred up a hornets' nest, as rapid Federal counter-battery fire forced the Confederate guns to be withdrawn, and a number of dismounted men from the 14th Virginia Cavalry had to dash back to safety. Some of the 5th Michigan Cavalry followed to an area around the Lott house.

As word of this meeting was sent back to Pleasonton, Custer was ordered to pull out of line and join Kilpatrick's post on the left. His place was covered by Gregg's brigade, led by Colonel John B. McIntosh. His men were in place by about 1 p.m. The two generals met to consider the situation and Custer offered to stay since the Confederates across the way appeared to be in large numbers. Gregg was happy for the support, and Custer stayed.

In the meantime, Stuart reinforced his line, placing nine cannon in position to renew the battle. Federal artillery also came into line, and an artillery duel began. After a short time, however, the Confederates, some of their guns short of ammunition, were forced to withdraw. At the same time, Federal cavalry moved towards the Rummel farm, defended by Virginia cavalry. Fighting was hard and neither side was able to budge the other. Stuart then decided to send his 1st Virginia Cavalry in a mounted charge. The grey cavalrymen entered the field east of Rummel's Woods just as Federal cavalrymen, out of ammunition, were pulling out. Although Federal artillery pounded the Confederates, the assault was successful.

Quickly Custer, whose command was divided into regiments specially trained in mounted charges, and regiments used as dismounted infantry armed with carbines, led his own 7th Michigan Cavalry in a counter-attack. The blue cavalry smashed into the grey, and the two split into small groups of flashing, swirling sabres. The Confederates, however, fled up the hillside as more Confederate reinforcements counter-attacked, some on horse and some dismounted, firing into the Federals from the Rummel farm area.

The Michigan Cavalry reached a fence running along the lane connecting the Rummel farmhouse to the Low Dutch Road. This stopped their charge, because they were now under fire from both flanks and the fence line. The 7th fled. But the Confederate counter-attack was in turn stopped by an attack by a battalion of the 5th Michigan Cavalry.

Now it was shortly after three, and several hundred of Wade Hampton's troopers moved onto the field on horseback, sabres drawn. Federal artillery soon had their range and tore holes in their ranks as they came on. At the same time, the 1st Michigan Cavalry drew their sabres and, led personally by George Custer, charged into the advancing Confederates. More troops of the 3rd Pennsylvania Cavalry joined the attack, and the Federals smashed into the Confederates, breaking up their charge. The Southern troops broke for the rear. With this, Stuart decided that his men had had enough; he had lost 181 officers and men. The Federals had lost 254. Stuart's attempt to take the vital intersection, one that cut the main supply line of the Union army and one of its possible routes of retreat, had failed. Later that evening the position was reinforced by infantry and fighting in this sector was finished for the day.

On the other flank, Kilpatrick had sent his remaining brigade, 1,925 officers and men in four regiments commanded by Brigadier General Elon Farnsworth, to an area south-west of Big Round Top. They arrived at about 10 o'clock and went into line on the Bushman farm, mostly in Bushman's Woods. The four regiments were supported by Battery E, 4th US Artillery, armed with four 3in Ordnance rifles. Farnsworth placed three regiments in line, holding the 5th New York Cavalry in reserve to support the artillery. Skirmishing went on along his line. Kilpatrick joined him with Merritt's brigade, less the 5th US Cavalry which had been sent to Fairfield, Pennsylvania, to capture a suspected Confederate wagon train.

Merritt's men went into line north of the Currens farm, and were supported by Battery K, 1st US Artillery, armed with six 3in Ordnance rifles. The Union line faced a mix of Confederate infantry, cavalry, and artillery. Young and impatient, Kilpatrick ordered a charge against this force.

Merritt's men went forward dismounted and in open order, every fourth man holding his own and the other three's horses, but after about fifteen minutes under heavy fire they were forced back. Kilpatrick ordered Farnsworth to make the charge mounted. Farnsworth was shocked, feeling that the rough terrain and stone fences behind which the Confederates were deployed would make such a charge very unlikely to succeed. His officers agreed and he went to Kilpatrick to get the order changed. Kilpatrick replied, 'If you are afraid to lead this charge, I will lead it.'

Farnsworth demanded that Kilpatrick retract this insult, and Kilpatrick did so, but continued to insist that the charge go ahead. Farnsworth returned to his men and made his preparations. His 1st West Virginia Cavalry were first out of Bushman's Woods and met heavy fire from rifle-muskets of the Texas Brigade. Then some of the mounted men jumped the fence and broke into the Texas line, sabres flashing, and the mêlée quickly split up into a series of small fights as the Union men, veering left and right, sought the safety of their own lines. They were followed by the 18th Pennsylvania Cavalry who came under heavy fire and the result was the same. Farnsworth himself then led the 1st Vermont Cavalry against Alabama infantry and, again, met heavy fire and losses. As Farnsworth rode towards the spur of Little Big Top he was hit five times and died on the spot. Kilpatrick's charge had failed totally.

Near Cashtown the 6th US Cavalry came upon the reported wagons on the Fairfield/Orrtanna Road and decided to charge them. Seeing that the train was guarded by the 7th Virginia Cavalry, the Federals dismounted half the regiment, keeping half mounted in the rear. Brigadier General William E. ('Grumble') Jones, the Confederate commander, decided to send in his troops mounted in a charge to clear the way. The dismounted Federal cavalrymen broke them up with heavy, rapid carbine fire, and Jones called up the rest of his brigade while a horse artillery battery arrived and came into line.

Before a second charge could be made, the Federal commander, Major Samuel Starr, had his mounted companies charge, and the fight became a close-quarters mêlée with pistols and sabres. Greater Confederate numbers eventually told, and the Federals fell back, closely followed by the enemy who stormed the dismounted cavalry line. The Federals, with Starr having been wounded in the fight, fled back to Fairfield, with losses of 60 per cent.

Towards 6 o'clock that evening Sykes ordered a brigade of Pennsylvania Reserves to advance from Little Round Top and clear Rose's Woods. The Pennsylvania troops cleared out skirmishers and a Confederate battery before running into the 15th Georgia, positioned in isolation along a ridge. The Georgians had no chance against an entire brigade, which soon swooped around their left flank and front. The Georgians fell back, rallying along a stone wall where they attempted to slow the Federal advance. But the Federals surrounded both flanks and captured most of the men and their colour. It would be the last action fought at Gettysburg.

5 AFTERMATH

Darkness fell at Gettysburg at about 7.30 and the fighting there was done. Members of the ambulance corps of both sides searched for wounded to bring back to the overwhelmed hospitals. Individual soldiers looked for fallen friends or simply made sight-seeing tours of the field – the first of millions who have done so ever since. Troops were assigned to bury the dead in their areas; the Federals doing so were first given a whiskey ration.

Shortly after sundown Lee called his senior generals to his headquarters. He said that the army would remain in position the next day, hoping that Meade would counter-attack and suffer heavy casualties as a result. If no counter-attack was forthcoming the army would withdraw to Virginia. Next day, under Lee's orders, Ewell's Corps moved to the right from its position, digging in on new lines along Oak and Seminary Ridges. The army's wagon trains, loaded with much in the way of captured supplies, and many captured horses, were started on the road south through the Cashtown Pass, through Greenwood and Greencastle, Pennsylvania, to Williamsport, Maryland, on the Potomac, where they would cross into Virginia.

'The army is in fine spirits,' Meade telegraphed Washington. 'I do not think Lee will attack me again.' Obviously still having defence in mind, Meade did not counter-attack, a decision that has been the subject of much heated discussion ever since. Hs generals agreed with his decision, Hunt speaking for most of them when he said he was 'right in not attempting a counter-attack at any stage of the battle, – right as to his pursuit of Lee'. Indeed, this was the general opinion of the corps commanders at a meeting Meade held with them on the 4th. Only Slocum, Pleasonton, and John Newton, then commanding I Corps, voted to leave Gettysburg, and even then they were against taking the offensive.

Back in Washington, away from the heat and smell of the field, officials were unhappy with the decision. Lincoln called it 'a terrible mistake', and Secretary of the Navy Gideon Welles thought Meade showed 'want of decision and self-reliance in an emergency'. Secretary of War Edwin Stanton felt that 'since the world began no man ever missed so great an opportunity of serving his country as was lost by his neglecting to strike his adversary'.

Unlike the previous three days, 4 July saw heavy rainfall on and off. Meade sent out reconnaissance parties; troops from XII and XI Corps found that Ewell's Corps was no longer facing them, and Howard moved into Gettysburg again. There they found a number of men who had been cut off in the first day's fighting and had been hiding in the town. They also picked up more wounded there. On the left, troops from V Corps moved from Little Round Top through the Wheatfield. They reported that 'Lee had refused his right flank, but was still holding a strong position toward the centre of the line'.

Federal cavalry under command of Major General William French, scouting from Frederick, Maryland, on the Potomac found and destroyed a Confederate pontoon bridge laid across that river at Falling Waters, and the cavalry, from Kilpatrick's command, captured some of the wagons of Ewell's Corps at Monterey Pass, near Fairfield.

On the morning of the 4th Lee sent a note through the lines to Meade suggesting an exchange of prisoners. Meade replied that he was not authorised to make such arrangements. In fact it would have been difficult for him to do so because he had had all his prisoners taken immediately to Federal prison camps so as to avoid having to tie down men in his rear to guard them. The Army of the Potomac didn't have a large number of prisoners in its area on the 4th. Lee also wrote a message to Jefferson Davis admitting that he had 'misjudged both the weakness of the enemy and the capabilities of his own army'.

Lee's infantry and artillery followed the wagons on the 5th. Hill's Corps led the way, followed by Longstreet's Corps, with Ewell's Corps bringing up the rear. Stuart's cavalry was sent by way of Emmitsburg to guard his left rear, while Fitz Lee's two brigades covered the right rear on the Cashtown Road. At 3 a.m. John Sedgewick had had his corps roused to reconnoitre their front yet again. This time they found no Confederates around the Emmitsburg Road or Seminary Ridge. Federal signal stations confirmed this, adding that the Confederates were not to be found anywhere on their old lines.

With that, early on 6 July, Meade ordered the Army of the Potomac to begin pursuit. The army would move as three wings, with Sedgwick commanding I, III and VI Corps; Slocum commanding II and XII Corps; and Howard with V and XI Corps. Each wing was to take a different route south and meet at Middletown on the 7th. The armies had left Gettysburg.

The armies may have left, but thousands of soldiers remained. The wounded from both sides who were unable to be immediately transported were left in makeshift hospitals in barns, buildings, and tents all over the Gettysburg area.

Meade's headquarters was in this frame farmhouse just below Cemetery Ridge, which forms the horizon. On 3 July Confederate artillery overshooting their mark on the other side of the Ridge did great damage to the building and wrought havoc among the horses in its yards. Meade was forced to flee during the bombardment.

George Stevens, surgeon of the 77th New York, recalled that, 'Our wounded were collected in great numbers in and about the field hospitals, which were composed chiefly of hospital tents, some farm house with its large barns, serving as a nucleus for each.' In all, 14,500 Federals lay in these hospitals.

And these were not all. As the Federal army slowly headed after Lee's troops, the medical personnel came across Confederate soldiers who had been too badly wounded to move. 'Every house and barn from Gettysburgh [*sic*] to Fairfield was a hospital; and about most of the large barns, numbers of dilapidated hospital tents served to increase the accommodations for the wounded,' Stevens wrote. 'All of the worst cases were left in these hospitals, the number being estimated, by the rebel surgeons in charge, at no less than fifteen thousand. Never had we witnessed such sad scenes as we were passing through today. The confederate surgeons were doing what they could for their wounded, but they were destitute of medicines and surgical appliances, and even food sufficient to supply those in their charge.'

In fact, the Confederates had left some 6,802 men behind in their field hospitals, making the US Army Medical Department responsible for more than 20,000 wounded men. However, the army's chief medical officer, Jonathan Letterman, creator of the army's ambulance corps system, had been told to expect another major battle when Meade caught up with Lee. Therefore, he left only 106 medical officers, out of the 650 in the army, to care for all the wounded (Stevens was one of those who accompanied the army rather than staying behind). Civilian volunteers, both local doctors and US Sanitary Commission members, flocked to the area to help, but they would be overwhelmed. Each doctor had 300 patients, but since only a third of all doctors left behind were operating surgeons, each one of those was responsible for 900 patients.

The Sanitary Commission set up a lodge at Hanover Station, the point where wounded were brought by ambulance or wagon and then transferred to trains. At first men were simply dropped there to await the next train, regardless of the weather. Soon, however, the personnel at this point were able to feed them coffee and soup, and had surgeons on hand to attend to their wounds, applying fresh dressings as needed. In all, 16,000 passed through this shelter on their way to hospitals in Philadelphia and Washington.

Many died needlessly. Most were buried originally in shallow graves, just to keep down the smell and contamination. But the government decided to set aside a part of the ground in Gettysburg as a permanent military graveyard. The dead were dug up, their pockets gone through to find any identification possible, and reburied in this graveyard, near the original town cemetery, on ground that had been fiercely contested. The Gettysburg Cemetery Commission was created to carry out this work, and they decided to hold a formal dedication of the new cemetery in November 1863. Their main speaker would be a man renowned in his time as an orator, Edward Everett. As an afterthought they invited President Lincoln to make a few remarks.

On 18 November Lincoln went to Gettysburg by train. He took time on the way to put finishing touches to the short speech he had prepared. That evening after dinner at the mansion of the head of the Cemetery Commission, David Wills, he was serenaded by the band of the 5th New York Heavy Artillery and afterwards asked to say something. Never comfortable in making off-the-cuff remarks, Lincoln declined, telling the crowd, 'In my position it is somewhat important that I should not say foolish things.'

The next morning Everett spoke for two hours, a long address given largely from memory and ranging from how slain Greek warriors had been brought back from battle on their shields to an account of the battle, given from material he had obtained from Meade. Then, as a photographer inserted his wet plate and opened his lens, Lincoln stood up and spoke the 272 words he had written. Finished before the photographer had a chance to get an image of him actually speaking, in these words Lincoln magnificently summed up the purpose of the war, and gave the nation as a whole a new direction and a new goal at which to aim:

'Four score and seven years ago our fathers brought forth on this continent a new nation, conceived in Liberty, and dedicated to the proposition that all men are created equal. Now we are engaged in a great civil war testing whether that nation, or any nation so conceived or so dedicated can long endure. We are met on a great battle-field of that war. We have come to dedicate a portion of that field, as a final resting place for those who here gave their lives that that nation might live. It is altogether fitting and proper that we should do this. But, in a larger sense, we can not dedicate – we can not concentrate – we can not hallow – this ground. The brave men, living and dead, who struggled here, have consecrated it, far above our poor power to add or detract. The world will little note, nor long remember what we say here, but it can never forget what they did here. It is for us the living, rather, to be dedicated here to the unfinished work which they who fought here have thus far so nobly advanced. It is rather for us to be here dedicated to the great task remaining before us – that from these honored dead we take increased devotion to that cause for which they gave the last full measure of devotion – that we here highly resolve that these dead shall not have died in vain – that this nation, under God, shall have a new birth of freedom – and that government of the people, by the people, for the people, shall not perish from the earth.'

The depth of the speech was not clear to everyone immediately. John Hay, one of the president's private secretaries who had accompanied him on the trip, said that his 'his half dozen words of consecration' were spoken 'in a fine, free way, with more grace than is his wont'. The strongly pro-Democratic, and hence Southern, *Chicago Times*, recognising that these few words changed the entire purpose of the war, called the speech 'a perversion of history so flagrant that the most extended charity cannot regard it as otherwise than willful'. Its competitor, the *Chicago Tribune*, however, was of the majority opinion when writing, 'The dedicatory remarks by President Lincoln will live among the annals of man.'

6
EVALUATING GETTYSBURG

The moment that the officers and men of the Army of the Potomac found that Lee's men had evacuated their lines they knew that they had won a major victory. 'The magnitude of the armies engaged, the number of the casualties, the object sought by the Rebel, the result, will all contribute to give Gettysburg a place among the great historic battles of the world,' staff officer Frank Haskell wrote shortly after the battle.

Major Charles Maddocks, 17th Maine, noted in his diary on 5 July: 'We are now in undisputed possession of the field; the enemy being reported 5 miles away in the direction of Cumberland Valley ... Bobby Lee will go home with his tail feathers out.'

Adjutant Charles Brewster, 10th Massachusetts Infantry, wrote home on 6 July: 'Deserters from the enemy have been coming in in squads all day, the enemy's force is supposed to be greatly demoralized ...'

Major Henry Abbott, whose 20th Massachusetts was in line near where Pickett's Charge crested, wrote home on 6 July: 'When our great victory was just over the exultation of victory was so great that one didn't think of our fearful losses.' His regiment's losses were indeed heavy, Abbott noting, 'of 13 officers, 3 killed, 7 wounded. Of 231 enlisted men, 30 killed, 84 wounded, 3 missing, total 117, with officers, aggregate 127.'

Army of the Potomac Provost Marshal Marsena Patrick noted in his diary during the battle that, 'Our losses were heavy, but the enemy's greater – Meade handled his Troops well ...'

Not all the men, however, were as sold on Meade's abilities. Captain Francis Donaldson, 71st Pennsylvania, which had been in the centre of the Confederate assault on the Clump of Trees on 3 July, noted in his diary on the 7th that Meade's general order congratulating his men 'upon their great victory' was read aloud. After that the regiment's colonel called for three cheers for General Meade: 'but not a man moved in response, not a voice was heard, all stood still ... No more cheering – there has been too many changes of commander, besides the army don't like Meade, they don't know much about him.'

Still, they had won the fight and beaten an enemy army that in previous battles always seemed to best them. Now they knew they could take on Lee and his Army of Northern Virginia and beat them. The Army of the Potomac that left the field at Gettysburg was not the same Army of the Potomac that had marched from defeat at Chancellorsville to Gettysburg. It would never be the same again.

Civilians who had been present at the battle, didn't know all this. They believed it when newspapers printed news of a total victory. 'Great and Glorious News! The Union Arms Victorious in the Greatest Battle of the Century!' headlined the account of the battle in the *Washington Star* on 4 July 1863. Only later would they learn of the human toll, but by then the impression of total eventual victory, reinforced by the surrender of Vicksburg on 4 July was complete. The Northern public would support the war with renewed effort.

Perhaps oddly, officers and men of the Army of Northern Virginia did not feel like a defeated army, however. Lee's adjutant, Walter Taylor, was greatly annoyed to read claims of a Northern victory. On 17 July he wrote to his brother: 'On the first day we were eminently successful ... On the second day we were also successful & drove them from a very strong position, capturing some cannons & many prisoners ... There was no opportunity whatever for a successful flank movement and on the third day two divisions assaulted a position a little to the left of their centre. Pickett's division of Virginians here immortalized itself. Its charge was the handsomest of the war as far as my experience goes and though it carried the works and captured a number of guns, it was not well supported by the division on its left, which failed to carry the works in its front & retired without any sufficient cause, thereby exposing Pickett's flank. The enemy then moved on Pickett's left & forced him to retire ... On the next day we waited patiently for the enemy to attack us. This they did not do nor have they at any time since either attacked or manifested any desire to attack us. They retired from Gettysburg before we did and only claimed a victory after they had discovered our departure.' Indeed, Taylor complained of Meade's 'lies about his *grand victory*'.

Confederate cavalry officer Charles Blackford admitted in a letter home written on 6 July that, 'Lee has fallen back and the campaign has failed, but nothing could be more orderly. There is not the least resemblance of a retreat except that we are counter-marching. The counter-march is as orderly, and Lee's orders about depredations are as well obeyed, as when we were advancing.'

Confederate War Department clerk J. B. Jones noted in his diary on 17 July that after many days of rumours, most of which came from Northern newspapers: 'At last we have the authentic announcement that Gen. Lee has recrossed the Potomac! Thus the armies of the Confederate States are recoiling at all points, and a settled gloom is apparent on many weak faces.'

Southern civilians were able to read between the lines. Robert Kean, head of the Confederate Bureau of War noted in his diary on 12 July: 'This week just ended has been one of unexampled disaster since the war began. Besides the surrender of Vicksburg and the retreat of Bragg behind the Tennessee river, which opens the whole Southwest to the enemy who now have two powerful armies opposed to two feeble ones, it turns out that the battle of Gettysburg was a virtual if not an actual defeat.' If Lee thought his Pennsylvania campaign would take pressure off Vicksburg and save that post on the Mississippi River, he was quite wrong, and the combination of his defeat and that city's loss was a major disaster.

Indeed, news of Vicksburg's fall coming on the heels of Gettysburg shook every Southern loyalist. Taliaferro Simpson, 3rd South Carolina Infantry, wrote home on 17 July: 'We have heard of the fall of Vicksburg. This is a hard stroke for the Confederacy. I will not say what I would like to say about national affairs, for the picture is too dark.' From this time on, desertions from Lee's army began on a more serious scale than ever before.

The real effect of Gettysburg is rather more complicated than either side's view. For years most people thought of Gettysburg as 'the high tide of the Confederacy', making the battle the turning-point of the war. More recently scholars have pointed out that if there was a single turning-point battle it would be Antietam, for that ended any serious chance of European intervention in the war and changed the war's purpose, in the view of outsiders, from being one to maintain the nation to one to free the slaves.

The battle was a turning-point for the Union armies in the east in that they would never again be as soundly trounced as they had been at Second Manassas and Chancellorsville. The psychological impact of the successful battle, especially when combined with the fall of Vicksburg, on Northern soldiers and civilians alike cannot be underestimated. But the Army of Northern Virginia was able to make up many of its losses and would go on to fight the Army of the Potomac to a standstill at places such as the Wilderness, Spotsylvania, and Cold Harbor.

However, Lee did manage to obtain several important results from the campaign leading up to the battle and his delaying actions thereafter. First, he did keep the war out of Virginia, allowing farmers to get their planting done and crops to grow unhindered, in the important months of June and much of July. He did capture massive quantities of supplies, and horses which were badly needed in the South. He seriously frightened civilians in far away Philadelphia, Washington, and even New York. In the end, however, he and his army were back where they had started.

Gettysburg, however, was a battle that continued to be fought in print. The first major controversy concerned Meade's lack of aggressive moves to attempt to destroy Lee's army starting on 4 July. Lincoln led those who disapproved of this, and many of the regimental level officers and men in the Army of the Potomac agreed. Meade, however, felt that to have done so could have threatened his ability to carry out the original orders he had been given: 'You will manoeuvre and fight in such a manner as to cover the Capital and also Baltimore.' Moreover, he had lost important corps commanders, Reynolds, Hancock, and Sickles, with two divisional and seven brigade commanders also casualties. Total losses were put at 23,000, 300 of these being officers, and his army was badly battered. The army had also lost so many horses that he immediately requested 3,500 more from the War Department. Meade and his generals agreed that a more aggressive pursuit was not a good idea.

Meade, however, would prove to be a careful general during the remainder of 1863's campaign in Virginia in which the two armies marched and countermarched in an attempt to achieve the best position for a battle that never happened. Neither he nor Lee could out-general the other.

Confederate controversies came largely after the battle. The first was the role played by JEB Stuart and his cavalry command. Moxley Sorrel, of Longstreet's staff wrote that he felt 'that the loss of the campaign was due to the absence of Stuart's cavalry'. The argument goes, since Lee lacked cavalry to determine the enemy positions and numbers, his infantry blundered into a battle that he was unlikely to win. In Stuart's defence, H. B. McClellan of his staff afterwards wrote that: 'Stuart carried but a portion of his cavalry with him, and that he left in direct communication with the army a force numerically superior to that under his own immediate command.' Certainly this cavalry was not used well nor did its commanders step up voluntarily to fill the gap left by Stuart. Moreover, McClellan claimed: 'Unless provided with an infantry support, Stuart could have made no reconnaissance which would have held forth any hope of piercing the cavalry which enveloped Hooker's advance.'

In fact, however, Stuart seems to have been more involved with bringing along the wagon train he had captured than in making a serious effort to reach Lee's main body in a prompt manner, and for this he must be faulted. He and Lee were apparently aware of his failure, Lee rebuking him on the field as he arrived, and Stuart taking some time to write a report filled with, at best, half-truths to defend his actions.

Ewell came in for immediate criticism for his failure to press the attack on Cemetery Hill on the evening of 1 July that Lee had suggested. 'It is exceedingly

The 1st Texas Infantry attacked across this five-acre field west of Devil's Den at about 4.30 p.m. on 2 July. The 124th New York counter-attacked from the stone wall in the foreground, and drove them back. In turn they were forced back by the 2nd Georgia, and the Confederates were able to cross the field and enter Devil's Den.

probable that, if we had moved promptly upon Cemetery Hill after the defeat of the enemy on the 1st, we would have gained the position, and thereby avoided the battle at that point,' Jubal Early wrote later. 'What might have been the result afterwards it is impossible to conjecture.'

Things looked differently on the ground that evening. Ewell's forces had been badly battered in fighting from Herr's Ridge, through the Railroad Cut and Gettysburg, and now the Federals had apparently established a solid line on definitely high ground. While Early argued that night to continue the attack, one of his other divisional commanders with whom he spoke that evening thought his men were too tired and footsore to fight and, besides that, he didn't think that such an attack 'would result in anything one way or the other'. Early was also aware that he had only a couple of battered brigades available since not all of his corps were yet on the field, and probably wouldn't be until well after dark. Years later one of Lee's staff officers, Armistead Long, who had personally reconnoitred the front, wrote to Early that, 'an attack at that time, with the troops then at hand, would have been hazardous and of very doubtful success'.

In fact, had such an attack been made and proved successful, what would have probably happened is that Meade would have concentrated his forces and then fought the battle on his chosen ground at Pipe Creek and won his glory there.

Longstreet, however, was the one who came in for the fiercest criticism from his war-time comrades in arms. Some of this came almost immediately after the battle was over. Lafayette McLaws, whose brigade attacked through the Peach Orchard, wrote to his wife on 7 July: 'I think the attack was unnecessary and the whole plan of battle a very bad one. Genl Longstreet is to blame for not reconnoitering the ground and for persisting in ordering the assault when his errors were discovered ... I consider him a humbug ...'

Most of the complaints about Longstreet's behaviour, however, came long after the war. In part this was due to the feeling that Lee's reputation had to be maintained, while Longstreet after the war crossed the political divide to join Lincoln's party. The battle was lost, Ewell and others afterwards claimed, because Longstreet failed to obey his orders, received from Lee on the night of 2 July, to attack in the dawn hours on the 3rd, at the same time as the attack was made on Culp's Hill. Instead, he dragged his feet, not calling up Pickett's men promptly and sending out scouts to hunt for a way around the Federal left flank. The attack was then delayed, and when made, not supported sufficiently to guarantee or even exploit success

In Longstreet's first defence, written by him in the 1870s, he side-stepped the question of having received orders, simply noting: 'I did not see General Lee that night. On the next morning he came to see me, and fearing that he was still in his disposition to attack, I tried to anticipate him ...' In his memoirs written even later, he claimed that Lee 'did not give or send me orders for the morning of the third day, nor did he reinforce me by Pickett's brigades for morning attack.'

This is simply untrue. E. Porter Alexander recalled visiting Longstreet's headquarters that night where he 'was told that we would renew the attack early in the morning. That Pickett's division would arrive and would assault the enemy's line. My impression is the exact point for it was not designated, but I was told it would be to our left of the Peach Orchard.' Apparently Longstreet, who had been against the previous day's attacks that had left his corps badly battered with precious little to show for it, decided to interpret his orders rather flexibly, giving him time to look for a way to make his favoured flank move.

Grudging, he did make the attack, but without doubt he failed to arrange for adequate support and failed to work with the units of Hill's Corps that were given to him. In his third account of the battle, written between his first and last account, he noted that he 'foresaw what my men would meet and would gladly have given up my position rather than share in the responsibilities of that day'. He offered to surrender command to Lee, who refused to accept this, something he should have done since Longstreet was in his own words convinced that the attack would fail. One has to feel that he did not do his utmost in preparing for supports for victory. Even his friend Sorrel wrote, 'There was apparent apathy in his movements. They lacked the fire and point of his usual bearing on the battle-field.'

In fact, it is unlikely that either Lee's charge or Longstreet's flank march on 3 July would have succeeded since Meade had the entire VI Corps on his left, ready to stop either move.

Hill stands alone as an uncriticised corps commander, yet he certainly failed here. He did not personally supervise any of the days' actions. He gave up troops to Longstreet yet failed to coordinate any movements or even his artillery for the third day's attack. His apathy is explained by his poor health during the battle, but it still cost the Confederacy.

Nor was Lee criticised openly by any but Longstreet, who paid for his words. Yet Lee allowed his army, blind as he knew it was, to be drawn into battle, then wasted his troops on attack after attack which he should have known, after Fredericksburg and Second Manassas, would be unlikely to succeed. He failed to meet Longstreet personally on the evening of 2 July to ensure that his orders were understood. 'Gettysburg has shaken my faith in Lee as a general,' Robert Kean noted privately in his diary. One of Lee's battalion commanders, Major Eugene Blackford, 5th Alabama Battalion, noted that his 'blind confidence in Gen. Lee is utterly gone,' adding that 'to hurl his Army against an enemy entrenched on a mountain top, it exceeds my belief'. These were words kept in private, however, and Lee generally was not as widely or publicly condemned for the defeat as Longstreet, Ewell, and Stuart.

In the end, however, when Pickett was asked who caused the South's defeat of these generals, he was said to have replied that he believed that the Yankees had something to do with it.

7
CONCLUSION

Gettysburg is one of those rare battles that combine high drama with results that definitely affected the war's outcome. Drama ranged from the smallest to the highest. Gettysburg native and Southern sympathiser Private Wesley Culp, coming back in his Virginia regiment to die on Culp's Hill, owned by his own family members. College professor Joshua Chamberlain, commanding the 20th Maine, having his men fix bayonets and charge to protect the Union left flank when they were out of ammunition. Pickett and Pettigrew taking their divisions across a vast field under enemy fire and nearly breaking the Union centre on 3 July. Longstreet and Lee bitterly clashing about the outcome of that charge.

Beyond the dramatic scenes, there were long-lasting effects. After Gettysburg nothing was ever the same for the participating sides. Southerners, military and civilian, were never again as confident in the Army of Northern Virginia. Lee realised that his army could not do everything he willed, while many of his soldiers realised that their leaders were capable of serious blunders. At the same time, Northerners, military and civilian, gained renewed confidence in their own Army of the Potomac. While it would be defeated by the Army of Northern Virginia in the future, such as at Cold Harbor, it would never take those defeats wholly to heart, remaining confident in its own abilities.

July 1863 brought Lincoln the generals he needed to win the war. Grant, the victor of Vicksburg, would become overall Union army commander. Meade, the victor of Gettysburg, would remain in command of the Army of the Potomac. As it turned out, Grant had more confidence in Sherman than in Meade and would

Barlow advanced his men ahead of the line to this knoll to his front, now known as Barlow's Knoll, on 1 July. In the foreground are gravestones in the Gettysburg almshouse cemetery.

choose to make his headquarters with the Army of the Potomac personally to direct its operations in 1864–65, although Meade would remain the actual army commander.

Lincoln was also given the opportunity, one which he rose to, of giving the definitive goal of the Union war effort, as well as a goal for all future Americans to aspire to, when he spoke at the military cemetery dedication at Gettysburg.

The shadow of Gettysburg hangs over almost every American. Novelist William Faulkner, son of a Confederate colonel, wrote in *Intruder in the Dust*: 'For every Southern boy fourteen years old, not once but whenever he wants it, there is the instant when it's still not yet two o'clock on that July afternoon in 1863, the brigades are in position behind the rail fence, the guns are laid out and ready in the woods and the furled flags are already loosened to break out and Pickett himself with his long oiled ringlets and his hat in one hand probably and his sword in the other looking up the hill waiting for Longstreet to give the word and it's all in the balance, it hasn't happened yet, it hasn't even begun yet, it not only hasn't begun yet but there is still time for it not to begin against that position and those circumstances which made more men than Garnett and Kemper and Armistead and Wilcox look grave yet it's going to begin, we all know that, we have come too far with too much at stake and that moment doesn't need even a fourteen-year-old boy to think *This time. Maybe this time* with all this much to lose and all this much to gain: Pennsylvania, Maryland, the world, the golden dome of Washington itself to crown with desperate and unbelievable victory the desperate gamble, the cast made two years ago.'

The result of Gettysburg. The larger stone in front of the rows of gravestones marked only with numbers indicates that 425 unknown dead of the battle are buried here in the Gettysburg National Military Cemetery, where Lincoln gave new direction to the war in his famous address.

SELECT BIBLIOGRAPHY

Contemporary Publications

McDowell, George. *The Union Almanac for 1863*. Philadelphia, 1863

Thomas, Robert B. *The Old Farmer's 1863 Almanac*. Boston, 1863

Official. *Regulations for the Army of the Confederate States, 1863*. Richmond, 1863

Newspapers

New York Times, New York, NY, 4 July 1863

New York Tribune, New York, NY, 29 June–7 July 1863

The Star, Washington, DC., June 15–6 July 1863

Star & Banner, Gettysburg, Pa., 2 July 1863

The Sun, Baltimore, Md., 4, 6 July 1863

Books

Acken, J. Gregory, *Inside the Army of the Potomac, The Civil War Experience of Captain Francis Adams Donaldson*. Stackpole Books, Harrisburg, Pa., 1998

Archer, John M. *Culp's Hill at Gettysburg*. Thomas Publications, Gettysburg, Pa., 2002

Beecham, R. K. *Gettysburg, The Pivotal Battle of the Civil War*. Longmeadow Press, Stamford, Conn., 1994

Blight, David W. (ed.). *When This Cruel War Is Over, The Civil War Letters of Charles Harvey Brewster*. The University of Massachusetts Press, Amherst, Mass., 1992

Bond, W. R. *Pickett or Pettigrew?* Butternut Press, Gaithersburg, Md., 1984

Brown, Andrew. *Geology and the Gettysburg Campaign*. Commonwealth of Pennsylvania, Harrisburg, Penn., 1973

Cleaves, Freeman. *Meade of Gettysburg*, University of Oklahoma Press, Norman, Okla., 1960

Coddington, Edwin B. *The Gettysburg Campaign: A Study in Command*, Touchstone, NY., 1968

Cole, Philip M. *Civil War Artillery at Gettysburg: Organization, Equipment, Ammunition, and Tactics*. Da Capo Press, Cambridge, Mass., 2002

Davis, Jefferson. *The Rise and Fall of the Confederate Government*. D. Appleton and Co., NY., 1991

Downey, Fairfax. *The Guns at Gettysburg*. David McKay Co., New York, NY., 1958

Early, Jubal A. *Narrative of the War Between the States*. Da Capo Press, New York, NY., 1989

Fishel, Edwin C. *The Secret War for the Union*. Houghton Mifflin, New York, NY., 1996

Gallagher, Gary W. *Lee & His Army in Confederate History*. University of North Carolina Press, Chapel Hill, NC., 2001

—*The Third Day at Gettysburg & Beyond*. University of North Carolina Press, Chapel Hill, NC., 1994

Gottfried, Bradley M. *Brigades of Gettysburg, The Union and*

Confederate Brigades at the Battle of Gettysburg. Da Capo Press, New York, NY., 2002

Hess, Earl J. *Pickett's Charge - The Last Attack at Gettysburg*. University of North Carolina Press, Chapel Hill, NC., 2001

Johnson, Robert Underwood and Buel, Clarence Clugh. *Battles and Leaders of the Civil War*, vol. III. Thomas Yoseloff, New York, NY., 1956

Jones, John B. *A Rebel War Clerk's Diary*. Sagamore Press, New York, NY., 1958

Ladd, David L. and Ladd, Audrey J. *The Bachelder Papers: Gettysburg in Their Own Words*. Morningside, Dayton, Ohio, 1994

Longstreet, James. *From Manassas to Appomattox*. Mallard Press, New York, NY., 1991

McClellan, H. B. *The Campaigns of Stuart's Cavalry*. Blue & Grey Press, Secaucus, NJ., 1993

McDonald, JoAnna M. *The World Will Long Remember*. White Mane, Shippensburg, Pa., 1996.

Martin, Dr. David. *Gettysburg July 1*. Combined Books, Conshohocken, Pa., 1996

Moore, Jerrold Northrop. *Confederate Commissary General*. White Mane, Shippensburg, Pa., 1996

Nye, Wilbur Sturtevant. *Here Come The Rebels!*. Morningside, Dayton, Ohio, 1988

Oeffinger, John C. (ed.). *A Soldier's General, The Civil War Letters of Major General Lafayette McLaws*. University of North Carolina Press, Chapel Hill, NC., 2002

Penny, Morris M., and Laine, J. Gary. *Struggle for the Round Tops: Law's Alabama Brigade at the Battle of Gettysburg*. Burd Street Press, Shippensburg, Pa., 1999

Pfanz, Harry W. *Gettysburg Culp's Hill & Cemetery Hill*. University of North Carolina Press, Chapel Hill, NC., 1993

—*Gettysburg – The First Day*. University of North Carolina Press, Chapel Hill, NC., 2001

—*Gettysburg – The Second Day*. University of North Carolina Press, Chapel Hill, NC., 1987

Racine, Philip N. (ed.). *'Unspoiled Heart', The Journal of Charles Mattocks of the 17th Maine*. The University of Tennessee Press, Knoxville, Tenn., 1994

Roach, Harry. *Gettysburg Hour-by-Hour*. Thomas Publications, Gettysburg, Pa., 1993

Rollins, Richard, *The Damned Red Flags of the Rebellion*. Rank and File Publications, Redondo Beach, Cal., 1997

Rozier, John, (ed.). *The Granite Farm Letters, The Civil War Correspondence of Edgeworth & Sallie Bird*, University of Georgia Press, Athens, Ga., 1988

Rollins, Richard. *Pickett's Charge!*. Rank and File Publications, Redondo Beach, Cal., 1994

Scott, Robert Garth, (ed.). *Fallen Leaves, The Civil War Letters of Major Henry Livermore Abbott*. The Kent State University Press, Kent, Ohio, 1991

Starr, Stephen Z. *The Union Cavalry in the Civil War*. Louisiana State University Press, Baton Rouge, La., 1979

Symonds, Craig L. *Gettysburg, A Battlefield Atlas*. The Nautical & Aviation Publishing Company of America, Baltimore, Md., 1992

Thomas, Dean S. *Ready... Aim... Fire! Small Arms Ammunition in the Battle of Gettysburg*, Thomas Publications, Gettysburg, Pa., 1981

Tucker, Glenn. *Lee and Longstreet at Gettysburg*. Morningside Bookstore, Dayton, Ohio, 1982

Wert, Jeffrey D. *General James Longstreet*. Simon & Schuster, New York, NY., 1993

—*Gettysburg – Day Three*. Touchstone, NY., 2001

Woodward, Steven E. *Davis & Lee at War*. University Press of Kansas, Lawrence, Kan., 1995

Philadelphia Weekly Times. *The Annals of the War*. Morningside House, Dayton, Ohio, 1988

Magazine articles

Bauer, Daniel. 'Did a Food Shortage Force Lee to Fight?', in *Columbiad*, vol. 1, No. 4

Bohannon, Keith. 'Wounded & Captured at Gettysburg, Reminiscence by Sgt. William Jones, 50th Georgia Infantry', in *Military Images*, vol. IX, No. 6

Crosby, James A. 'Those Three Days of Terrible Carnage: The Gettysburg Experiences of Lieutenant Alanson Crosby, Co. D, 154th New York Volunteers', in *Military Images*, vol. XLIII, No. 1

Hann, Scott and Herdegen, Lance. 'Attack and Counterattack', in *Gettysburg: Historical Articles of Lasting Interest*, January 1991

Hennessy, John. 'At The Vortex Of Hell', in *Civil War Times Illustrated*, January 1986

Hoffsommer, Robert and Mitchell, Robert Dale. 'The Rise and Survival of Private Mesnard', in *Civil War Times Illustrated*, January 1986

Jones, Terry L. 'Going Back Into The Union At Last: A Louisiana Tiger's account of the Gettysburg Campaign', in *Civil War Times Illustrated*, January/February 1991

Pohanka, Brian. 'Gettysburg: Fight Enough in Old Man Trimble to Satisfy a Herd of Tigers', in *Civil War*, Issue 46

Rollins, Richard. 'The Failure of Confederate Artillery in Pickett's Charge', in *North & South*, vol. 3, No. 4

Shoaf, Dana B. 'Death of a Regular', in *America's Civil War*, July 2002

Stefanon, Dyon. 'Pickett's Charge By the Numbers', in *Civil War Times Illustrated*, July/August 1993

Ronemus, Nancy. 'Eyewitness to War', in *America's Civil War*, March 1997

Ward, Eric. 'A Vermonter's Letter From Gettysburg', in *America's Civil War*, January 2002

Wert, Jeffry D. 'All The Powers of Hell Were Waked to Madness', in *America's Civil War*, July 2002

INDEX